THE HUNTER EQUATION

Secret Whisperings
From God & The Universe

THE HUNTER EQUATION

Secret Whisperings

From God & The Universe

By Brian Hunter

Published by
Rainbow Wisdom
Ireland

ISBN: 9781733811200

ABOUT THE AUTHOR

Brian Hunter is a well-known American psychic counselor, author, and life coach based in Los Angeles, California. Brian grew up highly intuitive, but after a major paranormal event, his abilities increased, and he shortly thereafter became a professional psychic.

Brian has been a member of Best American Psychics and was listed as one of the top 50 psychics in the world. Brian has worked with people from all over the world, including celebrities and captains of industry. Brian was an original cast member of the TV series pilot "Missing Peace," in which psychics worked with detectives to solve cold cases. He has also worked as an actor in Hollywood, featured in various Movie and TV productions unrelated to his psychic work. Brian's current work consists mainly of life coaching and counseling, but he also does psychic readings and works as a psychic medium, healer, and energy worker.

Brian is available for advisory sessions, lectures, and workshops, and is working on a series of books.

www.thehunterequation.com

CONTENTS

CONTENTS

CHAPTER 1

Who Am I And How Do I Know Anything?

elcome to this wonderful new prism, through which to view God, the Universe, Humanity, You, and all the amazing entities and energies surrounding us all.

This book is meant for everyone of all religions, no religions, spiritualities, political views, cultures, and backgrounds. I talk about many subjects, including some of the aforementioned. I want to make it clear that in no way do I mean any disrespect to any religion or belief you may hold sacred. In this book, I am very honest about presenting to you all my views, knowledge, impressions, and messages, which I have received from higher Universal sources. Some of these views may differ from your own. I suggest remaining open to my concepts and take in what resonates with you and your cultural beliefs.

But first, here is a little information about me. I am a psychic spiritualist who specializes in life coaching and counseling. I am an Empath, Psychic Medium, and Healer. I am also a teacher, advisor, consultant, and fixer. I have some experience and knowledge in the areas of psychology, medical, business, management, real estate, law, banking, working with children, adolescent counseling, hospice counseling, relationships, career development, and many other areas.

I started to realize my psychic abilities when I was 6 years old. I became lost in the woods and used my senses and communication ability with wildlife to find my way back home. Growing up, I was an excellent student, earning awards for my academic achievement. I have always been a self-starter and entrepreneur since my teens. I started mentoring young people at risk for suicide, and then counseling people of all ages and backgrounds. It was not long before I was listed by a publication as one of the top 50 psychics in the world. My primary interest remains my desire to improve people's lives through my life coaching work.

The reason I wrote this book stems from my responsibility to pass on all the knowledge and insights the Universe has imparted onto me. Most of the concepts in this book are from a higher power or source. I am merely presenting to you what I was shown directly by Source and the Universe. I also feel a compelling desire and responsibility to contribute toward human evolution any way I can. As teachers, that is what we do. My dream is for humanity to evolve and ascend to a higher state where all humans from all different beliefs, cultures, and backgrounds, can live in peace and prosperity. I believe this is possible with human evolution, as people develop a higher education, empathy, and moral values.

But the question remains, what makes me qualified to write a book like this? How would I even know any of the concepts I am about to present?

I have experienced intense paranormal events that have changed me as a person, deeply and forever. Among other things, I have had an "entity walk in event." This essentially gave me knowledge and insights from an outside source, which I never would have had. I also believe I have been subject to contact with life outside of our Earth realm. While some of these paranormal events were traumatizing and damaged me, they have also given me deep insights into all that surrounds us.

After my paranormal events, it was common for me to have lucid dreams where I was shown certain concepts of the Universe. I also have waking communications with higher Universal powers. You could say, "The Universe whispers into my ear." I believe I also have had various Spirit Guides trying to teach me and show me things. I have literally been on my exercise run and had mathematical equations or concepts come into my mind from nowhere. Sometimes I have words or thoughts pop into my mind randomly, which serve as hints of concepts to work on. I have been living for years like this, and thus have been exposed to many interesting ideas and pieces of knowledge, which I am about to pass onto you.

I consider myself very close to God, as I define God. I belong to no particular faith or religion, but am highly spiritual, and closely tuned into spirit guides, angels, and all that exists within the heavens and the hereafter. I believe Jesus existed as a historical figure and I look up to him for his love, inspiration, and mentorship. But with that said, I want to make it clear that I favor no particular religion, or even the concept of religion itself. I embrace all my Christian, Islamic, Hindu, Buddhist, and Jewish brothers and sisters, as well as those from all other faiths and beliefs, and embrace those with no faith at all. Thus, I mean no disrespect to any of the above, as I present in a very forthright way all the concepts that have been shown to me by the Universe. Please consider me a loving neutral party as I attempt to objectively present to you what I believe, and what I have been shown to be, the ways of the Universe. My hope is that the concepts and insights I am about to speak of, aid in human evolution, as well as each of you living a healthier, happier, and more successful life of your choosing.

CHAPTER 2

God And The Universe

Who is God, and what is the Universe? First, let me preface this by saying that I am not a scientist, astronomer, or physicist. Also, this is not a physics journal or textbook. My goal is to present my information and theories in a plain, linear, easy to understand, simple format. So, I am not going to get deep into the weeds, and I am not going to footnote everything I say. This book is about presenting my views and theories in a way everyone can understand. So, I will over simplify everything, and use layman's terms and explanations.

Wikipedia defines "God" as: conceived of as the Supreme Being and the principal object of faith. The concept of God, as described by theologians, commonly includes the attributes of omniscience (all-knowing), omnipresence (present everywhere), omnipotence (unlimited power), and as having an eternal and

12

necessary existence. Depending on one's kind of theism, these attributes are used either in way of analogy, or in a literal sense as distinct properties of the God.

Wikipedia defines the "Universe" as all of space and time and their contents, including planets, stars, galaxies, and all other forms of matter and energy.

Now for my own view and definition of God and the Universe, which has been whispered to me by higher sources greater than myself. I truly believe that God and the Universe is the same thing. They are two different words describing the same thing, and they are interchangeable.

I do not think the Universe is a dark space, and I do not think God is an old man with a white beard. I believe humans have been incapable of comprehending the Universe; thus, they have created a symbol or character for it. They have created "God" as a way to humanize, personalize, and clearly define "the maker" in human terms. The Universe made itself (will explain in a moment), and therefore is "the maker." The name God, or calling the Universe God, puts a human face onto the Universe. But the Universe is God, and God is the Universe.

I have always thought it weird, arrogant, and small-minded, how humans feel justified in "owning" everything in the Universe. In an infinite universe with undoubtedly countless solar systems, planets, and life forms, humans are convinced God is a human man. I think it is embarrassing to think like that. It is almost proof that humanity is very underdeveloped to be thinking in such short-sighted terms.

If God were actually a living being, he/she/it would most certainly not be human. God would likely be some other alien life form much more powerful and intelligent than a human. "He" would most certainly have to be an alien of some sort. God would also likely have no gender. But I do not think God is a living humanoid being. I believe God is the characterized human face we put on the Universe.

Science says the Universe was created 13.8 Billion years ago via the "Big Bang Theory." The Big Bang Theory indicates the Universe was formed from a Singularity, or single "event," or "explosion." Simply put, the Universe started as nothing from nothingness, such as from a black hole, where matter is infinitely dense inside a hole of nothingness. In a sense, everything is combined with nothing. I believe this push-pull may have collided with a random event or condition, which caused an explosion, releasing the infinite amount of matter out of nothingness, and into everything, which we call the Universe. Think of it as dropping a single pebble into calm water. Nothingness becomes an "event" (Singularity), where the water is hit, and then creates a wave of action which then emanates or spreads outward infinitely in the form of a wave of "something" (as opposed to calm nothing).

So, the big question really is what caused the nothingness to explode into everything. Physics has been desperately trying to determine this. In my own view, it was a Random Event, which mixed with the Singularity to cause the explosion, which resulted in the Universe. Math and the world of Physics will tell you that there is always a mathematical or scientific reason for everything. I disagree. I think there is a Random component to the Universe that cannot be quantified. Sometimes stuff just happens. No rhyme or reason. Humans are always desperate to have an explanation for everything because human nature requires it. But just because humans will not accept random events does not mean random events are not factually true. I think they are.

My Law of Randomality states: Events and circumstances exist within the Universe that cannot be predicted, explained, or quantified, by mathematics or science.

Let me give you an example of Randomality. Let's say there is a herd of zebras being hunted by a lion. The lion will indeed have a tendency to go after the smaller weaker zebras in the back of the zebra herd. However, there are usually several smaller weaker zebras on the fringes of the herd. What makes a lion decide to go after a certain zebra at a certain moment? Well, the lion is an organic thinking being. The lion has moods, urges, and compulsions. Due to these organic conditions, the lion's actions can be random. Based upon the random organization of the lion's thoughts, moods, and urges at that moment, the lion may attack at any given time of his choosing or instinct, or for reasons even the lion does not know. When he does attack, he will attack a certain zebra that happens to randomly be in a weak position at that moment. It is "bad luck" on the part of the zebra for being in the wrong place at the wrong time. This "bad luck" is random. If the lion was in the mood to attack a few minutes earlier, that zebra may have been in a different position and not been the one attacked. The positioning, timing, mood of the lion, and so forth, makes the event random. Thus, the lion randomly attacks one of the zebras he considers a prime target. The choice the lion made could have been easily changed by its mood, urge, or if the timing had the zebra in a different position earlier. Thus, the whole event is random. That zebra did not have to scientifically or mathematically be the obvious target of attack. It was just a random set of unfortunate circumstances which made that zebra the target of attack in that moment.

Also, no, I do not think the zebra signed a soul contract to come into this life to be eaten by a lion at that moment. It makes no sense and would serve the soul of the zebra no purpose. We have to apply some common sense to our situations, even if it would be tidier to just say the zebra signed a soul contract to be brutally eaten by a lion because he thought it would be fun and interesting to provide that important lion with sustenance.

There are many other examples I could give, such as why tornadoes destroy one home, but leave the home next door untouched. Had the slightest condition been different, a different set of homes would have been destroyed. I will not fill this book with random examples, but I am hoping you understand my point that randomness exists, thus my Law of Randomality. So therefore, Randomality also affects the Universe and all within it. As with the lion, Randomality is more common when involving organic forces. Organic forces would include anything living or any intelligent energy or matter. The Universe is full of energy and intelligent matter in my opinion. It is

15

this organic intelligence and energy which causes random behaviors, such as with the lion. I will be describing this organic intelligent energy and matter later on.

Anyway, my larger point is that I believe some random event interacted with the Singularity, which caused the explosion, releasing all matter outward like an ever-expanding ripple in the water.

So, picture an infinite amount of matter exploding outward from a single point. Like the ripples from a pebble, the matter continues to expand outward. Thus, the Universe is ever expanding. The Universe is ever growing, constantly expanding outward. Therefore, if you asked me how big the Universe is, I would not be able to tell you because the size of the Universe changes from second to second, since it is always expanding and growing.

This is where we come to my next concept. I believe everything is round. Everything is a sphere. Everything goes in circles. Everything comes around. Everything has a cycle that repeats in circles.

Everything I describe to you, whether it be the Universe itself, or the life cycle, it all is based on the fact that everything is a sphere, round, goes in a circle. It is a specific way of thinking, and you will see this theme in all my theories, views, and thoughts.

With this in mind, I describe the Universe as the inside of an ever-expanding balloon. Firstly, this means I believe the Universe, from our perspective, is concave. Meaning, we are looking at the inside of the balloon. All the contents of the Universe where we exist are inside the balloon. Outside the balloon is nothingness. The Universe is an ever-expanding balloon that never pops. The infinite amount of matter from which it originates guarantees that the balloon will never run out of matter or motion to continue expanding. The waves created by the pebble falling in the water will continue infinitely and will always be filled by an infinite amount of matter that came from the Singularity.

Therefore, I do believe there is a finite limited amount of space (volume) within the Universe, within the balloon. However, it is so huge and expansive, and ever growing (thus always changing volume), that it cannot be quantified, and will never limit us in any way. The inside of that Universe/balloon gets bigger with every moment.

Thus far we have covered what the Universe is, how it formed, and what its actual structure is. Before we get any further, let me revisit this idea that God is indeed the Universe and that they are one in the same thing. If you read the Wikipedia definition of God, you will see it talks about the attributes of God being omniscience (all knowing), omnipotence (unlimited power), omnipresence (present everywhere), and as having an eternal and necessary existence. These attributes given to God are identical to attributes the Universe has. This is because God *is* the Universe. People of faith have simply put a face on the Universe, so they can more easily relate to it on a personal psychological human level. It is the equivalent of calling the Earth "Mother Nature." There is no such person called Mother Nature. But humans wanted to put a relatable face on the Earth environment that they can relate to on a personal psychological level. I see nothing wrong with this, by the way. But it is important to point out these facts as a reality, so we see things clearly from a factual scientific point of view.

Now that we know what the Universe/God is, how it was formed, and its structure is the inside of an ever-expanding sphere, let us discuss the contents of that sphere. Scientists say the Universe contains Space, Matter, Time, and Energy. We will look at each of those items.

Space is all of the volume within the sphere we call the Universe. It can also be thought of as all the distance between the edges of the sphere, and the distance between the objects within that sphere. So, space is real, and we see it and know it. It is the volume of all the area around us and beyond.

Matter is all the "objects" within the Universe. These would be anything constructed with atoms, which is everything. So, Space is the volume of area, and Matter would be all the objects within that space.

Time is more interesting and complicated. Time is a concept, rather than a thing. Time has to do with distance and is a unit of measurement between one moment to the next moment. Moments do not all happen at once. Moments happen at different times, different intervals. *Time* is how we measure the different intervals. But here is where it gets interesting. Most humans think of *time* as linear, meaning a straight line from one point in time, to the next point in time. The timeline between January 1st to December 31st is a straight line. We move along this straight line through all the days, weeks, months.

With all this said, I believe *Time*, like everything else, is a sphere. What I mean is that I believe *Time* are little lines that wrap around the inside edges of the sphere. If this is true, then the lines of time must be round, because if you follow along the inside of the balloon, then you end up bending into a circle since the balloon is basically round inside.

I also believe that because the Universe is ever expanding, Time is also adjusting and bending to account for this expansion of the balloon, and growth of the balloon. Therefore, we will have some instances of time being imperfect. Time might bend. Time might also end up back where it started eventually since it is essentially a sphere.

So, on a micro level time is a very useful tool of measurement. Time is very accurate and reliable for measuring the passing of moments from last year to this year. It does not bend or alter. It is fixed. However, time on a macro level is very unstable and not fixed at all. On the grand universe level, time is always growing, expanding, and bending along with the concave insides of the balloon. Therefore, time can have imperfections and unexpected results we humans never consider.

For example, if we were to find one of these bends in Time, or irregularities in Time, we would be able to "travel" in time instantaneously. We could be in different Times, or maybe even more than one Time at the same time. I believe this is why humans on a deep intuitive level, realize that time travel might be possible.

Also, when people talk about traveling to different dimensions, or being in different dimensions, what they are actually saying is that they can be in a different Time within space. A different dimension is simply a different reality as defined by being in a different "time and space." So, if I can identify and exploit an imperfection or bend in *Time*, then I could certainly instantaneously be in a different dimension. Being in this different dimension puts me in a different time and space. It does this because being in a different time automatically means you are in a different space within the Universe.

I believe as we continue to explore the Universe, we will find such bends in *Time*. We already know Black Holes exist, and we know to stay away from them. We will also find bends in *Time* and we will know to stay away from them, or risk never being seen or heard from again.

The final content within the Universe is *Energy*. For our discussions in this book, *Energy* is the most important item, and the one we will be focusing on most. *Energy* has different meanings and there are different types, such as waves, etc.

Energy can be defined as a force, such as the energy (force) required to move an object. But Energy can also be defined as a collection of atoms forming an organic intelligence. This is the type of Energy we will focus on.

We psychics always talk about "energy", and "reading energy." We talk about this because as psychics, we actually feel, see, sense, and touch *Energy*. It is real to us, and consists of actual *matter*, made of particles. But what makes this particular *matter* interesting, is that it has a "life" to it. It has intelligence. We can sense feeling, thought, intention, and intelligence within this Energy. Somehow, this "object" of Energy is "alive". It is living Energy. It is a collection of waves, particles, and atoms that has organized into a mass of intelligence that we call *Energy*.

This *Energy* has life to it. What I mean by that is that it seems to contain life, intelligence, random movements, and intention. It seems to have some self-determination. The Energy behaves in forms of frequencies that can be sensed by psychics, or those who are sensitive enough to tune into the Universe or nature.

I believe this *Energy* is the "brain" of the Universe. I believe this

Energy IS God. This *Energy* is also what gives the Universe its random factor. Why? Because the Energy is somehow organic or alive in some way; and just like the lion, what is organic and alive, can behave in a random way.

Whereas the *Space* is the vast darkness, the *Energy* is the light. *Matter* is the body, and *Time* is the movement and distance. But I believe it is all controlled by the brain, which is the *Energy*. I believe the Energy consists of the souls and intelligence of all organic beings, or all intelligent life. But we will get into all this later, when we discus *Souls* in depth.

I believe this Energy, which is the light, is what people talk about when they have near death experiences and "go toward the light." When people talk about "going to God," they are talking about their soul reuniting with the light. They are reuniting with this collection of *Energy*, which I call the *Universe Energy Collective*. This is another reason I believe the Universe and God are the same thing. The *Energy* component of the Universe is what all of us go back to eventually. We go back home to God. We go back to the Universe Energy Collective.

Energy is the collection of Universal intelligence. It is the light. It is the brains of the Universe. It is the soul of the Universe. It is God.

I promise the rest of the book will not be this technical or complicated. Hang in there with me, as the fun is only beginning.

CHAPTER 3

Life Forms And Aliens

What life forms exist in the Universe? There are many. I challenge anyone to accurately define "life," and have that definition stand up to the test of time. Science is always making advances and I would guess things we do not consider "alive" now, we will consider "alive" or "life" in the future.

Let me give you one great example of this. Soul Energy. Soul energy from the Universe is something that does not require food, water, or sustenance, and never dies. Yet, I consider Soul Energy "life" because it is intelligent. Any entity with intelligence and self-awareness would have to be considered a "life form."

Conversely, let's look at grass. Grass is not thought to have any intelligence or self-awareness. Yet, grass is certainly a life form because it is alive and takes in sustenance, and eventually dies.

So, you can see trying to define "life" is a sticky wicket. Someday someone might say that rocks are life forms because they contain stored Universal Energy and can be unpredictable in how they move or react to certain conditions. I am kidding. But I'm not. So, I am not going to define "life" or "life form." But for the purposes of this book, I am going to consider "life forms" as anything organic *or* intelligent in nature. Examples would be Soul energy, Universal Energy, Plants, and animals. Obviously included as life forms would be humans and extra-terrestrial aliens.

I hope that last mention got your attention. This is not a book on biology, so we will not spend time discussing plants and animals. We have, and will again, discuss Soul Energy and Universal Energy. The book is really mostly about humans. But for this chapter, we need to discuss Aliens, or Extra-terrestrials. I do not want to seem politically or socially insensitive in how I refer to them. I apologize if any aliens reading this are offended at how I refer to them or terms used.

Now getting to the point, I find it arrogant and short sighted how humans always consider themselves the supreme beings at the top of the food chain, so to speak. If you read about the Universe, many would come away thinking that Earth is the only planet with life on it, and humans are the only highly developed life forms. Religions are all based on "God" being human form and serving only humans.

Are we really that underdeveloped that we believe this for real? Not about God or religion, but the fact that the Universe is all about humans, and only humans?

Scientists believe there are at least 100 billion galaxies in the Universe, with each galaxy having 30 billion planets. Notice I said "billion" in those numbers. The numbers are too big to comprehend. I cannot comprehend them. Humans cannot comprehend them. But the point is that surely any life form with an IQ better than a blade of grass, can deduce that there are advanced life forms out there other than just humans.

Thus, there must be aliens, extra-terrestrials. Fact.

So, the question is not about "if." The better question is "have aliens had contact with Earth yet?" I can say yes. You could say,

"Prove it." I might say "no," or "I can't," or "I won't." So, it is a debate we can have. Although you realistically cannot claim no aliens exist in the Universe, you could claim humans have not had contact with aliens yet, if you so desire to remain in that state of denial.

However, I personally am going to suggest that not only do aliens exist, but also that they have had contact with Earth; have had contact with humans and are among us already in some fashion. How do I know this? Well, I do not have an alien carcass to show you, if that is what you require. But I have had personal experiences which have led me to believe in their existence. Furthermore, I remind you of certain mysteries, such as the Egyptian Pyramids and other structures, which suggest more advanced life forms could have been on Earth in the past.

Anyone who knows me personally will tell you that I am a very logical, pragmatic guy that does not believe in bullshit. In fact, I have always been somewhat of a cynic when it came to psychic abilities and aliens. But life events and experience has taught me differently. I will give you some examples.

Firstly, I feel I have had direct contact with humans who have an alien component to them. What I mean by that is I feel there are humans who have been born with some alien interference or even alien DNA introduced into them.

Various children, teens, young adults and older adults, have told me stories of dreams they have had which are alien in nature. Meaning, they have had dreams that are not based in terms of Earth or humans. They are based on locations which are not Earth-like, and that include beings that are not human or Earth-like. In addition, some of these people exhibited some strange physical characteristics such as partial webbing of toes and bone ridges on their scalp. Skeptics could easily explain away such physical features, as well as the dreams. All I am doing here is sharing my personal observations and experiences. You can form your own judgments and beliefs.

Furthermore, I have had sessions with clients who claim to be alien

23

based. Now let us be honest and clear. Once again, I will be totally transparent. In some of these cases, I felt the client was delusional and had some mental health issues. But in other cases, I found them totally believable, and psychically and empathically, I sensed they were indeed "different." By "different" I mean they did not think or reason like a normal human. Also, their energy was very different from the energy of a human. It is possible they were just highly exceptional strange humans. But I am just saying they were very different, and it was conceivable to me that they were alien in some way.

Additionally, I believe I may have had an abduction experience personally. This happened to me many years ago while I lived in a home located in a very rural area on a lake. I will recall the event for you as I remember it, and you can draw your own conclusions.

As usual for wintertime there, I went to bed fairly early between 8:30PM and 9:00PM. I was feeling fine, was not ill, and nothing unusual was going on with me at the time. I think I must have fallen asleep somewhat quickly. The next thing I remember was waking up, opening my eyes, and seeing a huge bright flash of light outside my large picture window of my bedroom facing the lake. I had never seen a light like this before. It was huge and blinding. It was very momentary, and if I had opened my eyes a second later, I might have missed it.

Startled by the huge flash of light, I sat up and glanced at the clock. It was 10:02PM. I was expecting the clock to say 5:00AM or something like that. I felt like I had been sleeping all night. How could the clock be indicating I had only been sleeping for one hour? It was as if I was caught in some weird time warp. I sat in bed very confused. I was very disoriented, trying to figure out what the huge flash of light coming from the lake was, and why I felt like I had been sleeping all night, but had only been sleeping for one hour.

I ended up settling back down and falling asleep. I woke up at my normal time in the morning and went into the bathroom. When I got into the bathroom, I noticed something on my thumb. I took a closer look. There appeared to be a fresh puncture mark on the side of my

24

thumb. It was on my right thumb, and it was a tiny needle puncture wound with no blood.

It was one of those situations where logically I knew nothing had happened, and I just brushed it aside. But intellectually, I knew something had happened. I had a puncture wound on my thumb, a very bright flash of light, and a weird time warp effect. I can honestly say I had no negative effects and zero memory of anything. Whatever happened, it was done with amazing care and technology. I swept it all under the rug within my memory banks and went on with my normal life. Had I been abducted by aliens? My guess is yes. Feel free to disagree.

Finally, I feel it is simply logical that aliens have found Earth, are studying us, and have embedded within our society, for research and whatever other purposes. There are plenty of UFO stories that are credible as well. But humans are always afraid of what they do not understand. Humans react with denial and violence in such situations. It is highly likely that aliens are not necessarily scary looking green creatures with weird eyes. It could be that some aliens can be very human looking, or easily make themselves look human with DNA technology or cloning. They likely have no interest in killing us with death rays. They probably just want to live and learn like the rest of us.

Am I an alien? Or do I have an alien component to me? Well, I would not tell you if I was, or if I had. Why? Because if I told you that I was an alien, a few things would happen. First, you all would think I am a lunatic and I would be criticized and shunned as a crazy idiot. Secondly, you all would become very scared of me. Thirdly, I could no longer exist here peacefully for purposes of research or experience, because my "cover" would be blown. Finally, I would likely be lynched, captured, and killed, because that is how humans react when faced with things they do not understand. Think about it. If a human saw Big Foot in the forest, a human's first reaction would be to kill it and drag it back home, so he can show the world that Big Foot exists. It is human nature. So no thank you. This is why I do not think aliens will reveal themselves anytime soon. Humans will have to evolve more first.

I cannot stress enough that I believe aliens and extra-terrestrials play a big factor as life forms within the Universe. However, for the purposes of this book, I will be focusing on humans.

CHAPTER 4

What Is The Language Of God?

W hat is the language of God? This question is obviously also spoken as, what is the language of the Universe? Like all languages, we have to first decide who or what we are communicating with. Are we communicating with planets? Rocks? Dirt? Animals? Aliens? People? God? The Universe?

For the moment, let's all agree there is no point in communicating with inorganic non-intelligent matter. There is no point in having a conversation with a rock. I suggest we limit our consideration to all organic intelligent matter or energy. This would include people, aliens, animals, and God/The Universe. I include God and the Universe because it consists of Soul Energy, which has intelligence.

Now that we have limited our communication efforts toward organic and/or intelligent beings and matter, we need to figure out what form of language would be universally understood. Certainly, we know it's not English. Over half the people on Earth do not understand English, let alone animals, aliens, and perhaps some Energy. So, what is something all living or intelligent beings respond to?

LOVE

Show me anything that is organic and/or intelligent that does not respond to Love. It does not matter if it is a squirrel, cat, dog, human, alien, or energy, all of them would understand love.

What is love? Love is strong positive feelings and concern. If you show love, you also show compassion. If you love, you are willing to give of yourself for someone or something else. If I love, I give.

If I show love to an animal, I am peaceful and give food, comfort, and safety. If I show love to an alien, I would give something to them as a gesture, plus show safety, respect, and comfort. If I show love to Energy, I show it space, respect, and concern for its existence. Showing respect for existence can apply to anything. Anything and anyone, wants to see you will not harm it, that you are willing to let it exist, and that you are willing to give something of yourself.

So, if I run into an alien from the other side of the Universe, I need to immediately start communicating in the language of the Universe, also the language of God. Which is love. So, I will immediately respect its safety and right to exist. I will then give it something to show I am willing to give of myself for its benefit. These two acts would immediately show my intent to communicate peacefully.

I would act this way, no matter what. Maybe it is not an alien creature, but a blob of Energy, or invisible Energy, or sound. I would act the same in an effort to communicate in the Universal language of Love.

There is a caveat. The caveat is that this will not always work (snicker). For example, if I try to communicate with an angry bear this way, it is probably not smart. The same goes for a mean dog about to bite me. This is why we proceed slowly and gently. We are showing our peaceful intent, but we are also able to pull back quickly if needed. Communication with anything is always a risk. Sometimes we are hurt or rejected. But most of us agree it is worth the risk.

Hopefully I have now adequately prepared you to face an alien should you meet one. Communicate with Love. However, there are also some more sophisticated methods of communication that are worth mentioning. Music is a good method. Surprisingly, or not, most intelligent and organic beings respond to music. Sound organized in a harmonic way can convey organized thought and feelings. The only problem is that what one being thinks is great peaceful music, might be terrible aggressive music to another being. Symbols are also a method suggested. However, the obvious problem is that different symbols would mean different things to different beings.

Mathematics is a commonly suggested communication method. This would work for basic communication, but it is believed that humans are developed at such an inferior level, that our mathematics ability is only a fraction of what other alien beings, and Universal Energy itself, understand. So, speaking to the Universe or aliens with our mathematics might be the same as knowing only a few words like cat and dog.

In fact, I believe that Universal Energy operates under a very advanced and sophisticated system of mathematics, frequencies, and other things we do not even have words for yet. This is because Energy is not organic like humans and plants. Energy is eternal. With Energy, there is no organic matter involved that breaks down and dies, limiting its life. Therefore, Energy has had eternity to develop into highly advanced forms, which likely operate under highly advanced systems.

Many psychics feel communicating empathically (via telepathy) would be effective. This form of communication requires no words or sounds. It is communication using feelings and thought. This could work, unless different beings interpret feelings differently. For example, in human culture, we have something called "pleasure pain." So, the feeling is one of pain, but we humans like it anyway because it might be leading to some sexual arousal or other rewarding end. So, showing an alien "pleasure pain" might be interpreted as showing them "pain," harm, and aggression. Not good.

However, in most cases you will be communicating with humans. In your communications, perhaps keep in mind the Universal language of love. Practice communicating with the language of love. Even if you are angry about something, try communicating with love. A Master is able to communicate with love, regardless of the message being put forth.

Everything has its caveats, but most definitely the language of the Universe and the language of God, is Love.

CHAPTER 5

What Is Your Soul?

E verything in the Universe is related. Why and how? Because the Universe (everything) started as a Singularity. It started as one point of infinitely dense matter, which then exploded outward. So, *everything* relates back to that one single infinite collection of matter from the Singularity.

Therefore, as the Universe consists of space, matter, time, and energy so does the human being. The space is your volume and size, the matter is your actual physical body, the time is your aging process, and the energy is your soul and collective of your intelligence.

Some people might say, "I thought the human brain was the collective of the intelligence." Well sort of, but not really. The human brain is the organ that allows the body to function and live. The brain is also the collection of knowledge that a human learns through education. But the Soul of a person is the true essence of a person. The Soul is the collection of a person's eternal Energy.

Eventually, the body dies. With the body dying, the brain dies as well. But the Soul lives on because it consists of Universal Energy, or Energy from the Universe. The brain can die, but the Soul is eternal. This is the important point to remember.

We discussed in the previous chapter how amazing and magical the Energy component of the Universe is. The Energy of the Universe is amazing because it provides that organic living intelligence factor, which is also eternal.

So, what is your Soul? Your Soul is the collection of eternal Universal Energy within you. What does this mean? Well, it means many things. It means you literally have part of the Energy from the Universe inside you. You will recall I called Energy "the light" of the Universe. So, this means you also have "the light" within you. I also inferred that this intelligent Energy is also the essence of God, since it's the intelligence of the Universe. Therefore, you also have God within you.

You should begin to notice that most of what I have been saying does not conflict with many religious views. I am describing God in much the same way, and I am using many of the same terms used in religion, such as "God is the light," "Going back to the light," "going back to God," "God being with you or within you," and so on.

In summary, at this point of our discussion, your Soul is defined as the collection of Universal Energy that is within you.

The implications of this are very complex and far-reaching. Primarily, it means you have a part of the Universe's magic within you. You have a part of the Universe's intelligence and life within you. The fact this Energy is eternal makes it that much more interesting and amazing because it never dies and exists forever.

But next, there is a concept called "Soul Splitting" I want to discuss. This was a concept first introduced to me by famed psychic Andrew Brewer; and I have done my own work on it since, and in addition. Bear in mind that your soul consists of Energy particles from the Universe. This means your Soul as a whole consists of many

32

separate particles. It is my view that these particles do not always stay together in one place.

Let me give you an example. Let us say we have a bucket of water. The water is your collection of Soul energy particles. Let us say we dump out all the water and set the bucket aside. Indeed, most of the water will be all together exactly where we dumped it. But there will still be some trace amounts of water inside the bucket that we set aside. As you know, the bucket will not be bone-dry inside. The bucket will still have some drops or a film of water in it. Thus, all of the water that was once together as one, is now separated somewhat.

I believe the Soul energy particles may work the same way. Although most of the Soul energy might make it into the human body you are inhabiting, some amount of your soul energy particles, remain in the Universe with the larger collection of Energy we call the Universal Energy Collective. So, in a sense, some of your soul may actually be up in the Universe with the Universal Energy Collective at this moment. This would explain why some people feel a connection to some greater power outside of themselves. It could be they are tuning into, or sensing, their soul energy particles that are still with the Universal Energy Collective mass.

It is also possible part of your soul could be in another human as we speak. Let us go back to the bucket of water. We dumped out the bucket in one place. But maybe we noticed there was still a little water left in the bucket. So, we dump the bucket again, except in a slightly different location. Now your soul energy is in two different locations at the same time. Perhaps in two different humans at the same time. Not only that, but even after dumping the bucket a second time, there will still be trace amounts of water left in the bucket. Thus, you will still be partly with the larger collective of Universal Energy, in addition to being in two different places, and or people, at the same time. This might explain why some people feel a deep personal connection to another place or person. It could be that place or person is actually a part of you in the sense that part of your soul energy may be in that person.

From this point, we could even hypothesize that our Soul Energy is intermixed with many people and places, perhaps even infinitely. Perhaps this is why some people say, "We are all one." Perhaps we *are* all one. Perhaps all our Soul Energy is intermixed with an infinite number of people, beings, places, and the Universe.

The fact our Soul Energy is somehow connected to the Universe, and perhaps even other people and places, allows for an amazing opportunity. It means we may be connected to outside sources of information or intelligence.

I believe I am starting to outline a case for why and how psychics are psychic. Psychics have enabled their senses to tune into these other bits of Soul Energy. There are actually many reasons psychics are psychic. But this is one explanation. But I believe we are all capable of tuning into our Soul Energy, inside our body, and outside our body. I will be talking about psychic ability in detail later on.

Imagine the information and intelligence this Soul Energy contains. After all, it has been many places, infinite places. It has rubbed elbows with the Universal Energy collective, and it is eternal, thus it has been around for a very long time.

Consider this. We have established your Soul contains Energy from the Universe. The Universe originated from a Singularity, perhaps inside a black hole. Thus, a part of you was once a part of that Singularity inside a black hole as well. Imagine if you could tune into that information. Imagine if you could tune into the information contained within the infinitely huge Energy Collective in the mass of Universal Energy. Some people say you can.

There is something called the Akashic Records. Wikipedia defines the Akashic Records as: the Akashic records are a compendium of all human events, thoughts, words, emotions, and intent ever to have occurred in the past, present, or future. In other words, the Akashic records is the memory bank of the Universal Energy collective.

The only insertion I would like to make here is that I will be making a case as to why the Akashic records do not contain information of what will happen in the future. But for now, let us run with the general definition.

Now imagine Soul Universal Energy as millions of ants. All that Soul Energy divided up into people, each person being like an ant. People live their lives, learn, and gain knowledge and experience. Like ants, they travel around, but eventually travel back to where they came from. With them, they bring all the knowledge they gained from their travels. This knowledge gets dumped into the hive, which would be the large collective of Energy in the Universe. All this knowledge becomes part of the Akashic records.

So, the Akashic records is the library or the Wikipedia for the Universe. Imagine having access to this database. Well perhaps we do. If the Akashic records is part of the Universal Energy, and your soul is composed of some of this Universal Energy, then perhaps your soul has access to the Akashic records. Many psychics and deep thinkers feel they have some access or connection to the Akashic records. It would explain why some people have knowledge of things they have no logical explanation for having. People are often able to do mathematical equations or play instruments with no formal training or instruction. Some people are even able to write books on complex subjects even though they have no credentials in the fields of Physics, Math, or Science. How do these people do this? Perhaps they are tuning into the Akashic records or tuning into their Soul Energy.

Perhaps you can tune into your own Soul Energy. People are intentionally and accidentally doing this when they meditate. They are opening themselves up to sensing, and receiving information and intelligence from deep within themselves, and from outside themselves. This would be them tuning into the Soul Energy they have within, and their Soul Energy that is scattered outside of them as well.

My suggestion is that people consider recognizing their Soul for what it is and begin tuning into their Soul as a source of guidance, wisdom, and information. Humans already use their physical strength. Humans already use their brains. One of the next evolutionary steps of humanity will be to start using their Soul just like they use their physical strength and brain. The Soul is Universal Energy, and therefore is connected to the Universe and all the information the Universe contains.

CHAPTER 6

What Has A Soul?

In the last chapter, we talked at length about human souls. What I wanted to do here is expand upon the topic of souls a bit. Humans are arrogant self-centered creatures, and it is easy to forget that there might be other beings in the Universe who also have souls. So, let us ask, what has a Soul other than humans? I believe that any intelligent being has a Soul. By "intelligent," I mean a being capable of thought, feeling, and self-determination to some degree.

So, a robot that can "think," would not qualify to have a Soul since it cannot "feel." A robot also has no self-determination capability since it is controlled by its external programming. However, a squirrel has a Soul because it can think, it has at least some level of feeling regarding pain and urgency certainly, plus it has self-determination in that it can decide which tree it wants to climb first.

An alien would have a Soul because it likely has similar capabilities as a human, and then some.

Cats and dogs have a Soul because they are similar to a squirrel, except even more advanced.

Does a tree or plant have a Soul? Well, can a tree and plant think, feel, and have self-determination? Perhaps we do not have the answer to that. Science at this time would have a tendency to say no, because there is no brain or nervous system capable of thought. If science one day proves that trees and plants can think, feel, and have self-determination, then I will be the first one to claim they also have a Soul.

So, if something has a Soul, does this means when their body dies, their Soul Energy re-joins the Universe Energy Collective with all the other Soul Energy? Yes indeed. So essentially, in religious terms, does this mean all animals go to heaven? Yes, they do.

Does this mean an alien from another galaxy has Soul Energy within the Universe Energy Collective? Yes, it does. There are some of us who feel we have connected with such alien energy. Most humans do not consider such possibilities because humans in general only consider themselves within their limited human perspective.

Is the Soul Energy of cats and dogs up in the Universal Energy Collective? Yes. This is one reason why I and others believe that when we die, we can actually re-join our pets in the form of our Soul Energies reconnecting with our pet's Soul Energy.

Can Soul Energy from a human become Soul Energy of a dog? In other words, can human Soul Energy reincarnate into a dog? Yes, I believe it's possible. The reason why is because our Soul Energy has some self-determination. Our Soul Energy is on a mission and journey to have experiences, so that it may learn, grow, and evolve. If our Soul Energy determines that living a life of as a dog would be a great way to learn, grow, and evolve, then that reincarnation would be justified. I am not sure this actually happens all the time. Most likely, our Soul Energy desires to reincarnate into the most advanced beings it possibly can, in order to maximize the evolution process.

Can Soul Energy from an alien reincarnate into a human, and vice versa? Yes, it can, and I believe it does. When most people ask for a past life reading, they expect to be told they used to be some famous person, or that they remain the same gender in all past lives.

A woman wants to hear that they were Marilyn Monroe. A woman does not want to hear they were Charlie Chaplin. So, gender itself is an issue in doing readings for paying clients. So, imagine if you told a paying client they were an alien in a past life. They would freak out and want their money back.

When I do past life readings for people, I see many lives. Some lives as a human male, some as a human female, and some as an alien. I see them all. What I give the client is the one that comes through with strength, detail, and one they can mentally and emotionally accept. So, this means I almost always skip the alien past lives. But that does not mean they are not there.

When it comes to the question of what or who has a Soul, humans really need to start stepping back from themselves, and realizing they are not the only amazing creatures in the Universe worthy of having a Soul. There are many creatures and souls out there.

CHAPTER 7

The Cycle Of Life

Now that we have covered The Universe, God, and your Soul, let us drill down and begin to examine the Human Being. Certainly, the Cycle of Life could apply to any organic living thing. But for simplicity sake, we will just focus on Humans.

As I have said earlier, everything is round. Everything goes in circles. Let me first give you the example of the life cycle of water, since we have used water as an example before. We will begin our example by saying water starts in the clouds as vapor. When the water vapor gets dense enough, and other weather conditions permit, it then rains. The water vapor is born into water drops, which fall from the sky. The rain hits the ground and starts to soak into the ground or run off into the watershed. This means the water starts its long journey. The water might drain into some cracks and low-lying areas. Then the water drains into a small creek. Then it drains into a large stream. Then it might drain into a river. From there it drains into the ocean. Once in the ocean, with the sun heating it up, it starts to evaporate and turn into water vapor again, where it returns to the clouds, where it all started. So, the water began in the sky, was born into rain, had a very long journey on Earth, and then went back up into the sky. It is a cycle that repeats over and over infinitely.

Let's begin our human journey the same way. We start with our Soul Energy particles up in the light mixed with all the *Energy* of the Universe in the Universe Energy Collective. That is considered "home." It is home with God, and home in the Universal Energy Collective from whence it/we started.

Our Soul Energy is intelligent and has shared all of its prior information with the Akashic records. Our Soul Energy still mingles with its prior soul contacts, and with other Universal Energy, but our Soul Energy is ready for another adventure.

Why would our Soul Energy be ready for another adventure? The answer is because the purpose of life is to learn, grow, and evolve. The only way anything can do those things is by gaining more experience. So, if our intelligent Soul Energy wants to learn, grow, and evolve, it must gain more life experiences. One way to do that is to enter into another human life.

Meanwhile, back on Earth, we have two humans having intercourse and creating a new organic life through pregnancy. Two human life forms can create new organic matter, a new body, a new person, in this way. But it is just a body. The body still needs a soul.

A Soul can only come from Soul Energy. Soul Energy is found in the Universe, in the collective of Universal Soul Energy. So like rain watering a new plant to allow for it to live, Soul Energy finds its way down into a vacant organism (fetus), so that it can live and be a whole person.

I do not know when exactly this happens, just as I do not know exactly when a little seedling has enough water. In this book, I am not going to tackle the question of when a fetus becomes a person. That is for a different book at a different time. But once the Soul Energy has entered the fetus, that fetus in my view becomes "viable." An argument can be made though, that the "viable fetus" is still not a "person" until it is born and out of the birth canal. But again, believe it or not, I am not trying to start religious controversy with this book. So that discussion stops here. You can use your own belief system to *guess* at which point the Soul enters the fetus, and at which point a fetus is a person.

Although the Soul of the fetus is fully mature, the body of the fetus still has to fully mature. The cake has to bake before it can be taken out of the oven, even if the ingredients are already yummy. Okay, that was kind of a gross analogy. Or call it a swipe at humor. You get my point though. Even with an amazing Soul inside it, the body still needs to grow enough to be viable outside the womb.

The day finally comes, and the baby is born. It is definitely a full person now with its own body, mind, and soul. Let the adventure begin! But oh wait. Humans take a long time to develop. So again, even though the baby's soul is fully mature from many previous lifetimes and origins, the baby's body and mind are not even close to being ready for too much adventure quite yet.

So, the baby grows its body and develops its mind. The experience gained by the Soul at this point is minimal, but it is still there. There is still experience that can be gained through the love and attention the baby receives. Since the soul is fully mature, it can fully tune into everything, everyone, and all the energy surrounding it. So, the Soul takes in all of the interactions and stimulus that the baby comes in contact with. They could for example, experience the love, caring, and compassion humans can have for other humans who are unable to take care of themselves. A baby is totally helpless. But humans extend wonderful protection and compassion toward that baby to make sure the baby is okay. That is a wonderful, beautiful thing, and I am sure the soul takes all that in. There are always small nuances that can be experienced by such interactions.

42

The child grows older and can have interactions that are more complex. This allows for more challenging experiences. For sure, the soul is now able to gain the full benefit of human experiences it was hoping for before it left the Universal Energy Collective.

At this point, the full adventure is on! A child grows into an adult. An adult matures and lives out its life. The Soul is taking in all aspects of all the adventures. Just like the water running into the stream, then into the river, then into the ocean, the human journey progresses through many phases.

Eventually the human becomes old. The body starts to decay. The Soul is still vibrant and healthy. Most older people can attest to the fact they feel 16 inside, even if their body is much older. Older people still feel that spirit inside them. That "spirit inside them" is their Soul, which is in perfect condition.

Once the organic body becomes too old to function, the adventure for the Soul in that particular body is over. The process of death begins.

The body becomes old, weak, and sick. The same process holds true if the body is damaged or killed in some other way, such as an accident. The point is that the body is no longer able to continue as a viable host for the Soul. But for this example, we will continue with the assumption the body has become old, and the gradual process of death is happening.

The process of death can be an interesting magical thing. First, I will preface this by saying that for all the other people surrounding the dying person, it is very traumatic, scary, sad, and horrible. Humans do not like to lose their companions, friends, and family. Humans take loss very poorly. So much respect and acknowledgement, goes out to all of the humans who are hurt and suffer, due to the loss of the dying person.

But in this discussion of the life cycle, we are focusing on the one human and their journey. For that human who has lived their life and is now in the process of death, it can be a time of calm and introspection. The dying person is usually more concerned about

43

those around them than they are in themselves. There is a special reconciliation that happens within a dying person. There is a reconciliation between the body which is decaying and in pain, the mind which does not want to die but knows it is dying, and the Soul which is still in perfect condition and almost yearns to continue its journey in a more viable body.

If you look carefully, you can see this reconciliation within the dying person. They are clearly in pain and disrepair with a body that just cannot continue. That is easy for everyone to admit. The dying person is most often fed up with their body and does not want to deal with it anymore. The person is often accepting of the fact the body cannot continue and needs to die. However, this conflicts with the person's mind. The person's mind often does not want to leave, and feels concern for those being left behind, as well as business left undone, regrets, and challenges not completed. The mind is the one factor usually not wanting to die. The body is ready to die, but the mind is not. Then finally there is the Soul. The Soul wants to continue the journey, but in a body or host that can live fully in order to provide the maximum life experience. A body lying in bed for days is not of much use to a Soul wanting many experiences. The Soul also has its own intelligence remember. So, the Soul has mixed feelings of wanting to continue with the journey they have been on, but also wanting to "go back home" to the light of the collective of Universal Energy. The Soul also may want to start a new journey that is more vibrant. Therefore, the soul may feel reminiscent, but also ready to move on. All of these reactions and emotions can be observed within a dying person.

Eventually, the body goes into the end stages of death. The organs start to shut down. The mind starts to die along with the body. I believe there is a moment when the mind turns over all control to the Soul.

I have personally witnessed a person's death in detail. As a psychic, I was able to sense the person's emotions and thoughts during the entire process. I witnessed the body coming to a halt. Before that, I sensed plenty of brain activity. The mind was dreaming and reaching out. The mind was communicating with higher powers and spirit guides. The mind was receiving instructions and comfort on how to proceed. Then at a certain point, I no longer sensed any brain activity. However, I felt a strong sense of "being" as the Soul Energy was still intact and within the body. But very shortly thereafter, I saw and sensed the Soul Energy leave the body. I "saw" it in the form of an actual visible flash of light. I sensed it also, because after it was gone, the person felt totally dead and gone to me. Yet the person was still breathing. But not long after that, the person stopped breathing.

So, what I witnessed, was the body coming to a near stop, then the mind dying, then the soul leaving the body, then the body coming to a total stop.

In my opinion, death actually occurred the moment the soul left the body, because a body without a soul is not viable. This is why there is great debate as to whether or not discontinue life support for those who will not recover. As a psychic, my question would be to evaluate the state of the body, the state of the mind, and the state of the soul. By figuring out the status of those three things, I would have an opinion as to whether life support should be continued or not. Maintaining a body with no mind or soul is pointless and cruel. But I really do not want to digress off our current discussion too much.

So, the mind and body dies. The Soul Energy releases from the body. For me, the release is actually visible in the form of a flash of light. So again, the soul energy, the Energy of the Universe, is indeed "the light."

The Soul Energy travels up "to the light," "to God", "to the collective of Universal Energy." which could be called "Heaven." The Soul goes back home. The Soul Energy is now back where it started. The Soul Energy can intermingle with all the other soul energies and with the Universe Energy Collective from whence it came. The Cycle of Life is complete.

CHAPTER 8

Death: A Closer Look

I know we covered Death in the previous Cycle of Life chapter. However, there is always such intense interest regarding death, and many questions. In the Cycle of Life chapter, I really wanted to keep a clear balanced flow of the entire cycle without getting you lost in the forest or the weeds. Thus, I did not want to create an imbalance with an over-emphasis on Death, which is only one part of the Life Cycle. So, in this chapter we will take a closer look just at Death and hopefully answer some questions that were left unanswered when we discussed the Cycle of Life.

Birth and Death have many similarities. They are both well described by science. Birth takes Soul Energy from the Universe Energy Collective and puts it into a body, and Death gives Soul Energy back to the Universe Energy Collect from the body. They are both bookends to the Human Experience. However, when it comes to the Human Experience, one is the beginning, and one is the end. Humans do not seem as afraid of beginnings but are terrified of endings. Thus, most humans find Death terrifying. Why is this? Two reasons probably. First, because many see death as "the end." Secondly, because of the "unknown."

Death is the end of one particular life cycle. Human bodies only last so long, and eventually the body dies. The Soul never dies. Your Soul is eternal and jumps from one body to the next, to the next, or remains in the Universal Energy Collective. But organic bodies always eventually die.

So, when we say death is the end, we are only meaning the end of that particular human body. Plus, Death is only one part of the Cycle of Life. It is not "the end." It's one dot in the circle of "connect the dots." It is only one "item" in the process as a whole. Thus, I really only look at Death as being the end of a particular human body in one particular lifetime.

This seems a good time to insert a conversation about *Reincarnation*.

REINCARNATION

Reincarnation is the theory that we live more than one lifetime, and perhaps many life times. We keep coming back for more. Reincarnation makes perfect sense because our Soul Energy is eternal. Everything in the Universe is a sphere, because the Universe itself is a sphere. Everything is a circle. Everything runs in cycles. Plus, due to the principle of "Conservation of Energy," we know that Energy does not just vanish into nothingness. Energy disperses into other forms or places, but it still exists. Therefore, when a body dies, and the Soul Energy is released, that Soul Energy will still exist. So where does it go? When water evaporates back up into the atmosphere, where does it go? Does the water just vanish into nothingness? Or does it condense into clouds and once again fall to the Earth in the form of rain?

Soul Energy is like the rain. It has a journey on Earth, goes back up into the atmosphere (Universe), then comes back down to Earth. Everything in the Universe is recycled. Under the principle of "Conservation of Matter," matter never just vanishes into nothingness. It only changes form. What you bury in the ground either stays in the ground, or it turns into compost. But it still exists. It remains. So, everything is recycled eventually. Something might turn to dust quickly and end up helping to grow a tree. Or something might sit for hundreds or thousands of years before it composts and helps grow a tree. But eventually all matter is recycled in some way.

Soul Energy is recycled. Soul Energy leaving one life form, will end up as Soul Energy in another life form eventually. Granted, some Soul Energy may remain in the Universal Energy Collective. But even that energy plays a function and is being utilized somehow, and thus recycled. Reincarnation is simply the word used for the recycling of Souls. The recycling of Soul Energy.

Do we have a choice in whether our Soul is recycled? Yes and no. Our Soul consists of Universal Energy. That energy is intelligent. It learns, grows, has experiences, downloads to the Akashic records and interacts with the other energies of the Universe. Like most intelligent "life," Soul Energy has a factor of self-determination to it. This means Souls have some power of decision.

Remember, the purpose or goal of a Soul is to gain experience, grow, and evolve. The only way to do that is through experiences. A big way to get experiences is through living out a human life. So inherently, a Soul will at some point want to gain more experiences and will want to be recycled and reincarnated.

Does the Soul really have a choice? Ultimately, eventually, everything in the Universe is recycled or goes through a cycle of some kind. So, like it or not, Soul Energy will eventually be put to use somehow in some way. So, in that macro view, Souls have no choice but to be recycled or reincarnated. It is very similar to how humans have no choice but to eat. However, humans can choose when to eat

48

and what to eat. Humans can even choose to fast for a period of time. I believe the same type of choice exists regarding reincarnation and recycling. Some Souls may wait a period of time before reincarnating, while others may enter back into life form immediately.

Which is more enjoyable for Soul Energy? To be within the Universe Energy Collective, or inside a life form living out a lifetime? Well I am sure it is a matter of opinion but consider this. The Universe Energy Collective is certainly considered "home." It is where Souls begin and where Souls end. So, I can imagine "home" is where it is most comfortable. But like most of us, after we have been home a long time, we start to get bored and we get cabin fever. We lust for adventure and something new. This would be when a Soul would yearn to be within a life form living a lifetime. So, I think the ultimate answer is that a balance of both is best. "Balance" is usually a good answer to many questions involving the Universe and Life.

It is hard to talk about Reincarnation and not talk about Past Lives.

PAST LIVES

A Past Life is what the phrase suggests. Past Lives are the collection of lives, or lifetimes, we have had in the past. Our Soul Energy has been jumping from life form to life form since the beginning of time, except for any time it has remained in the Universal Energy Collective.

Usually we have very little connection or thoughts regarding Past Lives. Why is this? Well, our Soul is inhabiting a human body which only knows itself. Our body and mind only know the experiences they are having in *this* lifetime. Our brain was born with this body. Our mind is our intelligent word for our brain. They only live in this lifetime. However, our Souls have lived many lifetimes. But our Souls do not control our thinking. Our minds control our thinking. Our brains control processes and speech. So, everything our Soul knows, does not come out in the form of thought or speech. Therefore, most of us do not think about our past lives, nor can we talk about them.

With all that said above, our Souls do makes us feel things. Our Souls have a memory. Our Souls remember, and they feel. We can often feel our Souls deep inside on a spiritual level. As humans, we know what our heart feels is superficial but powerful. We know our brain sometimes rejects or embraces what the heart feels. But what we feel on a spiritual Soul level is never superficial. It is separate, deep, and permanent. This is how we know the Soul is separate from our mind and heart. Obviously, you will accept me using the term "heart" in a figurative way, meaning the sensitive emotional side to our mind.

Souls are able to make us feel or remember things in a vague way. Therefore, Souls can sometimes give us vague clues of past lives. Most people can relate to some of these weird vague feelings of familiarity with places, people, or events. We do not know where it comes from, but we know it evokes real feelings within us.

I personally have very deep and heavy familiar feelings regarding the Vietnam War, Vietnam itself, and music from that time. I have nightmares about it, dreams, feelings, and impressions. Yet, I was not a living functioning person during the Vietnam War. I have never been to Vietnam. I have had very little education or connection to the Vietnam War. So why are my feelings so intense on a Soul level? The explanation is that I could have had a past life that lived during the Vietnam War, and participated in it.

As a matter of fact, I am convinced I did have a past life in the Vietnam War era. I have had recurring dreams for years about my death. I have seen over and over in the same dream through many years, how I was wounded and then stabbed to death by the enemy. The meaningful part of the dream for me is how I knew I was going to die, and I was hoping they would stab me again and finish it quickly. It is horrible. I live it out with such detail and feeling each time I have this same dream.

Others have similar experiences and dreams. Others have unexplained fears about certain places and things. These illogical fears are likely a response to a deep Soul memory that we cannot explain.

While we have these vague feelings, memories, impressions, or dreams from time to time, for the most part we live out our current lives with little interference or knowledge of our past lives. It is probably best this way since we are supposed to be focused on gaining experience in this lifetime, rather than suffering from trauma due to our past lifetimes.

Why is it that so many people claim to be someone famous in a past life? For example, how many thousands of people claim to be Marilyn Monroe in a past life, right? Well first off, not all those people were Marilyn Monroe. Perhaps they wanted to be, or wished they were Marilyn Monroe, but clearly, they were not. However, let us not forget about our discussion regarding "Soul Splitting." Under the Soul Splitting theory, some of our Soul Energy could be scattered in more than one place or more than one body or life at a time. So perhaps Marilyn Monroe's Soul consisted of a collection of many different Soul Energies. So yes, it is possible more than one person could legitimately claim they were once Marilyn Monroe.

How does a psychic do a past life reading? Well of course, every psychic is different and has their own techniques and style. But in general, just like all psychic readings, a psychic will read your Energy. If a psychic can tune into your Soul Energy, they can access those feelings and memories contained within your Soul. This means the psychic can get impressions on the Energy they are reading. Through these impressions, a psychic might "see" an image, description, or feeling, of a past life. The psychic can then describe to you what they are "seeing." It might not be perfectly accurate, but indeed a good psychic can get impressions into your Energy which are revealing and interesting on a past life scale.

Is it possible some people have more past lives than others do? Yes. The reason for this is two-fold. Firstly, some Soul Energy may have spent more time in the Universal Energy Collective and less time in organic life forms. Secondly, some Souls may have had more lifetimes due to increased Soul Splitting. Thus, in effect, some souls are living two lifetimes while you are living one.

Obviously, entire books can be written on Past Lives, as well as Reincarnation. But let's move on and discuss in more detail the process of death itself.

I talked about the process of dying in the Cycle of Life chapter. So, let me jump ahead right to the moment of actual death. Let us say we have a human, who for whatever reason, is dying. The body is dying, and the Soul is transitioning back to the Universal Energy Collective.

I have seen this happen. As a psychic, it is fascinating to watch a person transition. Obviously, it is permanently traumatizing on the highest level if it is a family member or close loved one. But as a professional who works with clients and associates, I was able to witness it from a more detached third-party perspective. I alluded to this story previously, but I will tell it in its full detail now.

His name was Larry and he was someone I had worked with on a professional level, so I knew him fairly well. However, we had fallen out of touch and I went months without any contact with him. One day I received a message from a close friend and associate of Larry. She informed me that Larry had been diagnosed with terminal cancer and she thought I should know. She told me he was presently in hospice, and where. The next day I made a trip up to the other side of town to see Larry. It was indeed a hospice facility. The front desk told me which room he was in. I found the room and walked in. Larry was lying in bed half unconscious, with oxygen and tubes coming out of him. I was horrified and shocked. I was obviously way too late for a proper visit.

But when I walked closer to him, he woke and saw it was me. He seemed really surprised and I said, "Hey Larry." He responded, "Hey Brian, how are you doing?" There was something funny about it because he was acting like everything was normal and totally fine, as if we were meeting on the street or something.

I told him I had only heard about his situation recently and that I was sorry. I knew he had bone cancer and clearly, he was very end stage. Then Larry said something under his mask. He said, "Heal me. Try." I gulped because, um, it looked a bit late for that. But I took his hand and focused. What I "saw" in my mind was a body completely littered and covered with tumors and cancer cells. There was seriously no way. But I acted as if I was giving it a good college try as a way of showing Larry I cared enough to try. I knew he was dying. So, I thought to myself that if I cannot save him, maybe I can help him with his passing. I became determined and looked at Larry and said, "You won't have to do this alone." "I will come back." "I will come back in a few days." "You need to hang on until then." Larry nodded and motioned to me goodbye and I left.

In my car on the way home I contemplated when I should return. The psychic message came in very clear. "Thanksgiving Day." Thanksgiving was about a week away and I actually had no plans for Thanksgiving that year. So, I waited until then.

The morning of Thanksgiving I drove up to Larry. I was hoping he would still be there, if you know what I mean. Sure enough, he was. I walked in, and he seemed both surprised and relieved I was there. By this time, he could no longer speak. I could tell he knew it was me though, and he could understand when I spoke to him.

I told him it was good to see him and that I was honored to spend my Thanksgiving with him. I am not a touchy-feely guy, but I took Larry's hand and just held it, as if praying with him. I was trying to tune into him and determine where he was at with his process, and how close. I could tell he was very close to the end. So, I started talking to him. I told him it was going to be Okay. Then I just started launching into my "instructions" on how to "do this." I told him to relax. I told him that if at some point he felt an urge to just "push off," that he should gently "push off." I told him I would be with him and guide him to the light. He seemed to truly focus on what I was saying and be determined to follow my instructions. That day Larry fell in and out of consciousness. I could tell when he was in pain, and I would get the nurse for more morphine. I also had to have his oxygen turned up regularly all day until it was on full blast.

During my day with Larry, his daughter showed up, who I had never met. I introduced myself to her and explained what I was doing. I told her that if she preferred privacy and wanted me to leave, that I would do so with no hard feelings. She enthusiastically asked me to stay. We visited and got to know each other, and we bonded.

I monitored Larry all day and into the evening, making sure he got his morphine shots. I observed him closely and stayed tuned into him. He woke up momentarily when his daughter was there, and they had a moment together, but then Larry was out again.

Eventually I could tell Larry was fading. I could sense he was seeing things and interacting with someone, or some presence. I could sense he was very close, and he was "talking" to whoever was basically "meeting him" at this point of transition, is what it felt like to me. My senses were much heightened, and I even told his daughter that I thought it was close.

Larry got "quiet" psychically, and I watched him. I am pretty sure I sensed the "push," or he was trying to push up. For some reason, I felt like I was intruding, and I looked the other way, almost as a way of giving Larry some privacy. A minute or seconds later, I turned my head to glance over at him, and I saw this huge flash of light. I was a bit startled by it. I immediately asked his daughter, who had been watching TV in the room, if she had just seen that flash of light. She indicated she had not. But I was sure of what I saw. I got closer to Larry and looked at him. I tried to sense him. Nothing. He was still breathing slowly, but I could not sense any brain activity. He was gone to me.

I explained to the daughter what I felt just happened and I told her I felt he was gone. We kind of had a moment and I just stared at him. We had a nurse come in and check on him, and he was still breathing, but he was totally cold and barely had a pulse. I stayed another hour, and then I really felt I should leave. I really felt Larry was gone. I felt Larry no longer needed me because he was actually gone. I felt him push off, I saw his soul leave his body, and I sensed his soul meet the light in spirit world or the Universe Energy Collective, or in religious terms, Heaven. It felt complete to me. I asked his daughter if she needed me to stay. She indicated it was okay if I left. I said my goodbyes to her and left. Shortly after I returned home, his daughter texted me saying "He stopped breathing and it's over. Thank you, Brian."

I want to acknowledge Larry in this book and thank him for allowing me the gift of witnessing his transition. Larry always liked being the star of the show and I think he would approve of us all learning from his experience of transitioning from human life back into Soul Energy within the Universe.

Let's talk about some of the points of the process I witnessed with Larry.

How did I know which day Larry would die? I read his energy. As a psychic, I received the message and impression of "Thanksgiving Day." You can call it a guess or a hunch, or a good psychic read. But to me, it is about reading energy and listening for psychic messages.

Did Larry have some choice in which day he passed? Yes. Certainly, a person can choose to "fight on" or "let go." Larry was dying for sure, so there was a limit to how long he could wait. But as long as I showed up in a reasonable amount of time, Larry was able to "hold off" his transition by choice. It is a matter of remaining engaged and fighting, as opposed to "letting go" and "pushing off" when the opportunity arises. Life is full of stories about how elderly couples both die within a short period of each other. The human mind, along with the Soul can conspire to have an influence on such things.

Who was Larry talking to in his mind shortly before he passed? I believe our Souls can communicate with other Soul Energies. I discussed previously how during death, the brain/mind ends up yielding control to the Soul as the mind shuts down and dies. Therefore, the Soul is in control of the brain and can communicate with other Soul Energies in such a way that the person can for the first time "see" and "hear" these communications which previously could only be "felt." Larry was communicating with Soul Energies that he felt very close to, and perhaps were going to comfort him or even "accompany" his Soul Energy back to the Universe

Energy Collective. These other Soul Energies can also be described as loved ones we were close to who previously died, or soul mates, or other significant soul contacts we had.

So, does our mother, father, sibling, or deceased spouse, meet us at death? Well, according to the above paragraph, yes, they can.

What was the flash of light I saw leaving Larry? The flash of light was his Soul Energy, or his Soul, leaving his body. Soul Energy is the light of the Universe. It makes sense it would appear as a flash of light to a psychic.

Why didn't Larry's daughter see the flash of light? I do not know. She was watching TV at the time and maybe was not paying attention, or it could be that I saw it only because I am psychic. It might be similar to a dog whistle, where only a dog can hear the whistle. An average human can't hear the whistle. Maybe psychics are more tuned to see "the light."

Did Larry go to be with God? Yes, he did. Larry's Soul Energy went back to the Universe Energy Collective. Back to the light. Since the Universe is another word for God, Larry indeed went back to God. Larry went back home.

Is Larry in Heaven? Yes, Larry went to Heaven. Heaven is the place we go after we die, correct? "Heaven" is a word for the Universe Energy Collective. Heaven is where we are truly comfortable and surrounded by love and peace. Most certainly, all Soul Energy feels comfort, love, and peace, being back home surrounded by other Soul Energies in the Universe Energy Collective. That is Heaven.

Why was Larry still breathing after his Soul left his body? You will recall that when pregnancy occurs, there is a fetus but no Soul Energy. Same thing when you die. There is a body, but no Soul Energy. Larry's body simply existed a bit longer after the Soul Energy had left. The body and the Soul are two separate things and can exist separately for a period of time, although a human is not viable without a Soul.

By the way, when I was driving back home after leaving Larry upon his soul energy exiting, I received a psychic message from him. The message was "Thank you." This to me meant he was already able to communicate with me from the other side.

How can a psychic communicate with the dead? The answer, as before, is that a psychic can tune into, and read energy. A psychic can sense Soul Energy. Therefore, a psychic can tune into that Soul Energy and receive impressions or messages from that Soul Energy.

How does a psychic know which energy to tune into? For example, how do I know to tune into your deceased Aunt Mary's energy? Different psychics have different techniques. Some need a name. Myself, I need a photo. Psychics just need some trace item, so they can tune into the correct energy. It's like you giving me the frequency of the radio station you want me to listen to.

Can a psychic communicate with a person or soul that has then reincarnated again? Yes. Soul Energy is always connected to the Universe Energy Collective in some way. Souls have a direct connection, but also, through Soul Splitting, there is a likely a trace amount of the person's soul still remaining in the Universe Energy Collective, even if most of their Energy has reincarnated into someone else. In theory, you just need one particle of Soul Energy to fully communicate, since all the Energy particles share all the information and intelligence. This is analogous to how we only need a tiny hair of a person to get their entire DNA sequence since the DNA is shared throughout the entire body. We will discuss psychic abilities in more detail later on.

Is there life after death? As you can see, yes there is. Only the body dies. The Soul is eternal and lives on forever. The Soul not only lives on in the form of Energy, but also lives on in the form of future reincarnations.

Can you travel around, visit people, and see what is going on after you die? Yes, you can. Since you consist of Energy (of light), you can most certainly travel at the speed of light to anywhere. I also believe you can travel faster than the speed of light by bending time and switching dimensions.

Can you communicate with people after you die? Yes, but only if they are able to receive your messages. They would have to be somewhat psychic and open to recognizing, tuning into, and listening, to the frequencies of your energy.

Can you be in more than one place at the same time after you die? Yes, you can. This is because of Soul Splitting. You can be in as many places at one time as you have particles of Energy. If I had a million particles of Energy, I could be in a million places at once by splitting up all my energy particles to go separate places.

Being dead sounds amazing and wonderful, so why would I want to be alive? Read the chapter later in the book called "The Human Experience." Despite all the limitations of being human, there are amazing experiences and sensations that can only be enjoyed as a human. I could also say being a collection of Energy particles also has its limitations. That is why the Universe offers diversity and balance.

I mentioned at the beginning of the chapter that the second reason Death was scary to people was because of the "unknown." I am hoping I have addressed that part of the equation by making the death process less unknown.

CHAPTER 9

The Hunter Equation

I just spent a lot of time talking about Death. I think now it's time we talk about how we live. Much of the remainder of the book will be discussing the various philosophies by which humans live and exist.

Humans like to think they live in their own bubble they entirely control. There are many philosophies and books written on how a human can get anything they want by thinking or doing certain things. All humans by nature want to have total control over their environment, their circumstances, and their future. Humans will buy anything and do anything, which they believe will give them this magical power to control their fate and get anything they want.

The "Law of Attraction" is a perfect example of a philosophy millions of people have bought into thinking they can bring positive outcomes into their life simply by thinking positive thoughts and bring negative outcomes into their lives if they think negative thoughts. Can a person really control their outcome by what they think? Is it that simple? Have you tried it?

Or is there more? Is the Universe more complicated than that? Is life more complicated than that? Like many people, I spent plenty of time contemplating all of these questions.

When I was a teenager, I read many motivational books based on the power of positive thinking. I was very interested in becoming wealthy and successful back then. I was young, full of energy, and highly motivated to do anything I needed to do in order to achieve "success." The books I read all preached how I must think positive 100% of the time and "fake it until I make it," meaning "pretend" I am successful even if I am not. Or in other words, live a fantasy in my mind that I already have what I want, even though I do not have it yet.

I did find these books to be motivating. They made me feel better. They made me feel like I was already successful and already made it to the Promised Land. They made me feel like I would achieve all my dreams. I enjoyed them a great deal. But did the books make me successful? Did I achieve all my goals and dreams from thinking positive thoughts and having wonderful fantasies in my mind?

No. I ended up achieving a certain level of success mostly from keeping my goals in mind, staying focused, working very hard and persistently for many years, and by leveraging my contacts I met along the way. I also took full advantage of opportunities offered and found. Finally, I must admit I also got lucky in some things.

Honestly, it was not easy. By the time I had achieved anything, I had long stopped reading all those motivational and positive thinking books. I was exhausted and too busy juggling all the aspects I mentioned above. No one thing worked. Even just working hard was useless. A person can work hard for years and accomplish little. A person can think of their goals every minute of every day and still accomplish little. A person can try to use their contacts and coat tails to succeed, but without some substance behind them, they will not get far. Then there is always the luck factor that brings both good luck and bad luck. We have all heard of and seen people get lucky in business. It happens.

So how does a person succeed? How should a person live? How should a person think? How can a person survive in this world of endless complications and problems? Why can't life just be easy, where I think what I want, and I get what I think?

Well first of all, humans have to get off their high horse and get over themselves. Humans are but small creatures within the Universe. We do not control the Universe. The Universe controls us. More accurately, we as humans are all part of the Universe. We are one cog in the machinery.

I have talked about how I see the Universe in structure and in operation. I have shown how humans have a cycle within the Universe and are a part of the Universe. It seems to me that the most logical approach to success is for humans to better fully understand their place in the Universe and how they can best interact with the Universe.

I am trying to say in a very polite way that humans do not exist in a bubble. Humans exist as part of the Universe, and with the Universe. Humans do not control everything, however much we wish that were true. Humans do not control the world just by using their wishful thoughts. Sorry to break that to you. Grab a tissue if you need one. Instead, humans play a part in the Universe and are free to react with the Universe and everything within it.

Do not worry, I am not here to simply debunk everything you thought you knew and leave you more confused and discouraged than when you started. As a reminder, ever since I experienced my traumatic paranormal events that changed me forever, resulting in accelerated psychic abilities, I have had whispers from the Universe coming into my head for years. I am that guy at the grocery store buying fruit, and all of a sudden have an epiphany about how the world works. I have equations, ideas, and concepts constantly streaming through my head out of nowhere. I literally think that way and live that way most every day. But some epiphanies are bigger or more significant than others.

One day, I had one such epiphany while out for my run. At the time, my regular run included running up to the top of this holy mountain. You might not consider it a holy mountain. It is not on the map of the most holy places, or on any map for any reason actually. But it is a place where I have done lots of energy work. It is a magical place to me. I have felt the energies up there and tuned into them. I have been inspired up there. I have performed healings and other miracles for people up there. It is holy to me.

But anyway, one day I was running up the mountain and I had one of my epiphanies. I had been wondering for a very long time "how the Universe works," in connection to how humans can successfully engage with it. I had long become cynical of the positive thinking books and the Law of Attraction. I was looking for the real answer. I was not looking for something that sounded clever and easy. I was looking for the Truth. What is the True Truth on how things work? Please tell me the Truth even if it is not good or easy. I asked this of the Universe.

Finally, I received an answer on this one day. I was shown a written equation by some higher power of the Universe. It was like a whisper in my ear, along with a visual in my mind. Therefore, I cannot claim that I sat down writing equations and one day I figured it out myself. I was given this by a higher power, so I am not going to claim full credit.

Keeping that in mind, please forgive any perception of arrogance as I introduce to you what I call "The Hunter Equation."

The Hunter Equation states that a person's Future Outcome is determined by four elements: Intent, Actions, External Forces, and Random Luck.

The Hunter Equation:

Future Outcome =
(Intent + Actions + External Forces + Random Luck)

Let's discuss each of the elements.

Intent: Intent refers to your intentions, attitude, goals, and thoughts. The Law of Attraction people should at least be happy with this element. Clearly, your future does indeed depend somewhat on what you intend to do. This, therefore, could be considered a Free Will element. You must clearly decide what you want to do and put some thought to it. Some persistent positive thought does not hurt. But I do not even think it has to be positive thought, as long as it is a strong intended thought which you remain fixated on while you work to achieve it.

Actions: Actions refer to actions you actually take toward a certain goal, outcome, or future. Just thinking something does not make it happen. A person must take actions to physically make it happen. Of course, actions can also be bad things. If a person performs bad actions, then that will contribute to a bad result and bad future outcome. Actions are very powerful. Actions can very quickly result in very bad things. Actions can also result in very good things. I have observed that bad actions seem to have more immediate results than good actions though. Again, life is not easy. So, Actions are critical. Actions are obviously considered another Free Will element.

External Forces: External Forces refer to all those pesky environmental or circumstantial limitations, people, or events that are outside our control that affect our outcomes. Regardless of our Intent and Actions, External Forces will always be there to provide obstacles or total blockages. External Forces tend to limit us and cause us problems. However, External Forces can also help us. For example, a good External Force might be a mentor or powerful person who actively helps us achieve something that we could not have achieved on our own. Therefore, a clever person will find a way to use External Forces as positive leverage in helping themselves. External Forces are often limitations and road blocks, but they are also short cuts and

63

opportunities. The key point on External Forces is they are outside our control. External Forces are things we mostly have to react to, rather than plan and control.

Random Luck: Random Luck is that element I introduced earlier into our discussions of the Universe that make life interesting and scary. Random Luck acknowledges that some things are truly outside our control. If I am trying to get a certain job, it truly does depend on what day and what mood the boss is in when he reads my resume. I cannot control what day, what hour, or what mood the boss is in when he happens to pick up my resume. It depends on total dumb luck. It's random. Sometimes people, companies, or the Universe, simply has to flip a coin to see which person gets something. and which person does not. It's random and luck. It has nothing to do with what you deserve, what you think, what you did, or your circumstances. It just depends on random luck. Some days it goes in your favor, and other days it does not. Anyone who has won a huge prize in a lottery understands random luck. They know they did not earn it, or even deserve it, or even do much to get it. All they know is they got lucky and were randomly chosen. Hopefully they are at least grateful. So fortunately, or unfortunately, random luck will partly influence your outcomes and your future.

A melting pot of these four elements is what I think determines a human's outcome and future.

Does one element have more power than others do? I do not know. I wish I had a definitive clever answer for you. But I would be lying if I said with authority that I knew. Again, I can only profess to know what I have been shown by the higher powers of the Universe. I was shown the equation. I was not told if the elements had different weights. Personally, I live my life assuming they all have equal weight. Realistically, for the most part, they do I would say. I say this because each element is so critically important, that one element can easily throw off all the others. So, for that reason, I would personally

64

theorize that all elements have equal importance.

Not to make this more complicated, but it is slightly more complicated. I was shown there is another layer to the equation. The equation repeats itself under each element. This means that under each element, all four elements exist again. Perhaps it is easier I show you this way below:

Future Outcome =
(Intent + Actions + External Forces + Random Luck)

Intent	Intent	Intent	Intent
Actions	Actions	Actions	Actions
Ext Forces	Ext Forces	Ext Forces	Ext Forces
Luck	Luck	Luck	Luck

So, what I am saying above is that under each element, also lies all four elements again. Let's take Intent for example. The element of Intent includes Intent, Actions, External Forces, and Random Luck. To drill down on this example, let us say for a moment that you are creating an intent of achieving a certain goal. While you are creating that Intent, you need to consider the literal Intent, obviously. But you also need to consider the actual Action of creating the Intent, plus any External Forces affecting your Intent, plus the fact that Random Luck will play a role in your Intent.

Hopefully that is not too confusing, but now let us use the element of Action as an example to hopefully provide more clarity. Let's say you are deciding on Actions to attain your desired Future Outcome. While you are considering what "Action" you are going to take, you need to consider the Intent of each Action. This adds another layer of validation that the Intent of your Action make that Action correct. You also need to clearly define the Actions required behind the general Action you are taking. Then you need to consider all possible External Forces that might affect your Action. Finally, consider what part

Random Luck may play in your Action.

In short, the four basic elements determine your Future Outcome. Additionally, when constructing your plan for each element, you must also consider all four elements for each.

Nobody said the Universe was easy. Nobody said life was simple. Nobody promised you a rose garden. But if you take the time to truly understand The Hunter Equation, and truly understand each of the four elements, and how to apply each element, you are very close to the Truth of how your Future Outcome is determined. Once you understand and accept this, it becomes easier to use this equation and its elements to your greatest advantage. Do not worry, I will talk more later in the book about how to apply the equation to your life for maximum desired results until it is crystal clear.

CHAPTER 10

Destiny Vs. Free Will

Spiritualists argue over the question of Destiny vs. Free Will. Do we sign some contract before birth to live out some pre-determined destiny? Or are we born to do with our life whatever we decide? Do we have total control over our future? Or is our fate sealed and there is very little wiggle room? What is Destiny? First, let me preface by saying I may use the words Destiny and Fate interchangeably. The two words might have different connotations to some people, but for the most part, they can be used interchangeably. Wikipedia defines Destiny as: Destiny, sometimes referred to as fate (from Latin *fatum* – destiny), is a predetermined course of events. It may be conceived as a predetermined future, whether in general or of an individual.

Destiny means we have a set future that we cannot change. Some Spiritualists say we agree to a life contract or soul contract, before we enter a new life, and we agree in advance to everything that is about to happen to us. These Spiritualists claim that if I step in front of a bus at age 10, it is because I chose to do that in advance of being born, and it was meant to be.

Spiritualists defend and support their views by the fact that many people define the Akashic records as including everything that will happen in the future. Meaning, the Akashic records not only contain everything that has happened, thought, and learned, but also everything that *will* happen. This would infer that the future is already decided, and is already written, and just needs to be played out. Our culture is full of references to the fact that many believe our futures are about Destiny.

In how many films and books have you seen or heard the phrase "It's your Destiny." The first thought in my mind is Darth Vader standing over Luke Skywalker proclaiming, "It's your destiny." Of course, he is referring to how Luke is supposed to join the Dark Side, overthrow the Emperor, and lead the Dark Side.

But *was* it Luke's destiny to do this? Or were these just the words of an evil narcissistic father trying to brainwash Skywalker? If I tell you "It's your destiny," perhaps you will believe me, and do what I say because you are convinced you have no choice, since your fate is sealed? I do not know about you, but Destiny is starting to feel more like a "tool" someone would use to manipulate another person into doing something.

It is hard to imagine that an unpredictable organic living being could have a set Destiny. That this freethinking being could have a set future that cannot be changed no matter what they do. Does that make sense to you? If this were true, then why would be bother doing anything? If our fate is sealed and future destiny laid out, why would I even bother going to work? If my destiny is sealed, then I can just lay on the couch and eat cookies instead of working.

Plus, I have already talked about how there is a random factor to the Universe. If this is so, then a pre-determined future would be impossible. You cannot have a set future if random things are happening as you go. This is the reason I disagree with the official definition of the Akashic records. You will recall the Wikipedia definition of Akashic records to be: The Akashic records are a compendium of all human events, thoughts, words, emotions, and intent ever to have occurred in the past, present, or future. It is the part of the definition indicating that the Akashic records contain records of what happens in the future, that is a problem for me. Clearly, since the future is not fixed, it is impossible for there to be records of everything happening in the future. So, I am suggesting a revision to the Akashic records definition to remove any reference to Akashic records knowing everything that will happen in the future.

Additionally, why would a Soul want to live, grow, evolve, and experience things, if it already knew the end of the story? What would be the point of the Universe entirely if the end is already written? Why would the Universe be expanding if the future is determined already? Also, how can a future already be set in stone while the Universe is ever expanding?

There are too many variables and constantly moving parts for there to be a set ending, or pre-determined future. It is logically impossible. Physics and Mathematics would say a set ending is impossible with constantly changing variables and exponentials in effect. It also goes against common sense.

So, what about Free Will? Wikipedia defines Free Will as: Free will is the ability to choose between different possible courses of action unimpeded. Basically, it is pretty clear that Free Will means a human has complete full control over all events. Notice the word "unimpeded" is used. That definitely means no limits, exceptions, or caveats.

Therefore, under the Free Will theory of life, Spiritualists say that a person has full control over their lives. A person can decide what they think and what they do. A person can create any outcome or any future by actively choosing it. Now we are getting into "Law of Attraction" territory.

A Free Will Spiritualist would say you first decide what you want your future outcome to be. They would say you have full control over your future, so tell me exactly what you want your future to be. Then, you would set that intention clearly in your mind. You would only think positive thoughts focused on that intention. Then you would take actions that support that intention. They claim if you did all this correctly, you would eventually get your desired outcome. Or, in other words, your future would turn out exactly as you intended it. Or, in other words, you just had full control over your future and created your own future from entirely your own Free Will.

The only problem with this inspiring motivational theory is that reality and real life gets in the way. Darn it, don't you hate it when that happens?

What happens is things do not turn out exactly as you had planned or hoped. The narcissistic Spiritualist that guaranteed this technique would work, then blames its failure all on you. They will say that your intention must have been unclear, or weak, or not specific enough. They might say your focus must have been too weak. They might say that a negative thought must have slipped into your mind at some point, thus destroying your mojo. They will have 100 reasons to say it is all your fault, and that the Law of Attraction and Free Will method is still absolutely true and correct.

Are we really going to buy into that? It sounds like snake oil to me. Do not tell me a certain method is God's truth, when in fact it is impossible to follow, and when I fail, you are just going to blame it all on me, and still declare victory for yourself.

The truth is that nobody has total Free Will. You already know this. Anyone over the age of 30 knows this. Anyone who has fought like hell for something and done everything possible to get it, yet failed to get it, knows what I am talking about. Sometimes things just don't work out despite our best efforts. If Free Will were as easy as deciding what we want, thinking positive thoughts, and taking action to get it, then we would all be doing it and succeeding, yes? I mean come on. Most of us reading this have busted our behinds for things and failed. One important lesson we teach our kids is that we do not always get

70

what we want. That does not mean we should not try. It just means failure and disappointment is part of life. Accept it, brush yourself off, try again, and never give up. Life is not easy. Why is life not easy? Life is not easy because none of us have absolute Free Will.

We all have limitations. We are limited by being human, first of all. Some of us have academic limitations. I suck at math, so it is not likely I could use Free Will to become a rocket scientist. Others are blind, so it's not likely their free will would allow them to become a brain surgeon. We all have physical and mental limitations as a result of being human.

We also have environmental limitations. We have circumstances that limit us. It would be hard to use my Free Will to become President of the United States when I am a poor child born in Africa. We all have these environmental and circumstantial limitations that prevent Free Will. No amount of intent, positive thinking, or actions are going to eliminate all human, environmental, and circumstantial limitations. Limitations are part of the Human Experience. Due to limitations, Free Will is impossible. So Free Will is not happening. Sorry.

To sum up, we live in a world where philosophers and Spiritualists argue whether we live a life of Destiny or a life of Free Will. In reality, both Destiny and Free Will are impossible and debunked. I am going to go under the assumption I have done a fair job of invalidating both Destiny and Free Will. You are free to disagree, but under the circumstances, and my supporting evidential arguments, I have to move on assuming Destiny and Free Will is not an option. Neither of them is a Universal Truth.

So, what now? Should I just leave you hanging here? Should I leave you with more questions than you had before you started reading this chapter? Of course not! From the previous chapter, you probably already know where I am heading with all this. Neither Destiny nor Free Will is the answer, because neither of those are based on all four elements of the Hunter Equation.

As a reminder, here is the Hunter Equation again:

The Hunter Equation

Future Outcome =
(Intent + Actions + External Forces + Random Luck)

You cannot just throw your hands up and leave everything to Destiny. Nor can you have the arrogance to think you decide and control your fate. Your future actually depends upon the four elements of the Hunter Equation, which are your Intent, Actions, External Forces and Random Luck.

Does this mean there is no such thing as Destiny or Free Will? No, actually both still exist. However, they exist with less importance, as only a part of the whole. Destiny can certainly be confused with what will happen to you through Random Luck. Free Will certainly has plenty to do with the Intent of what you decide, and the Actions you take. So, elements exist, but they are not the entire picture, and therefore not complete Universal Truths or Laws.

Your future outcome relies on The Hunter Equation.

CHAPTER 11

Synchronicities & Soul Mates

S o, what is a Synchronicity? Wikipedia defines a Synchronicity as: a concept, first introduced by analytical psychologist Carl Jung, which holds that events are "meaningful coincidences" if they occur with no causal relationship yet seem to be meaningfully related. During his career, Jung furnished several different definitions of it. Jung defined synchronicity as an "acausal connecting (togetherness) principle," "meaningful coincidence", and "acausal parallelism."

So, a Synchronicity is a coincidence yes, but it actually rises to a higher level than just a coincidence. A Synchronicity is a coincidence with some accompanying evidence, justification, or contains multiple layers of coincidence. For example, it would be a coincidence if you and I showed up at the same place at the same time. But if we showed up at the same place at the same time to buy the same thing, *that* would be a Synchronicity because that has multiple layers of coincidence.

In this chapter I ask for your leniency, as I am including several different topics that may not simply be Synchronicities, but I wanted to include them in this chapter because I feel they are either related to coincidence or Synchronicities, or they should be, or they are mislabeled as a coincidence or Synchronicity.

Also, let's have some leniency in using the words Synchronicity and Coincidence interchangeably, but we all know now that a Synchronicity rises to a higher level than a single Coincidence.

So, how do coincidences and synchronicities happen in the Universe and in our lives? Who makes them happen? Does God and the Universe make them happen? Do you make them happen? Are they part of some pre-ordained design? Or are they manifestations we directly cause? Oh, what a mess of questions. What a tangled knot we have here. We will now go about untying this knot by picking at one section of it at a time.

The first step in doing this, is invoking The Hunter Equation. We do this because Synchronicities are basically a question of Destiny or Free Will because we are asking who creates them. Does God and the Universe create them (Destiny?) Or do we ourselves create them (Free Will)? Answering the question of who creates them might lead us to figuring out how they are created and why.

In the previous chapter, we already determined there are no valid laws of Destiny or Free Will. Both of them only exist partially in some circumstances. So rather than such matters being either Destiny or Free Will, the Hunter Equation states that these matters of Synchronicities are a product of (Intent + Actions + External Forces + Random Luck).

Using the above equation, how does a coincidence or Synchronicity form? Well, indeed they partly occur from our Intents, our desires, dreams, goals, wants, needs. But they are also a result of certain Actions, such as what jobs we take, places we go, where we live, who we choose to communicate with, and so on. External Forces also play a role, in that we may be forced into a Synchronicity by the fact of

74

where we are working or living or things we are obligated to do. Finally, coincidences and Synchronicities can also be partly a result of just being in the right place at the right time as dumb luck would have it.

Thus, Synchronicities exist from a varying combination of the above four elements of the Hunter Equation. So, anyone who says Synchronicities are only from God, or only you are manifesting them, can agree or disagree, but you will know for sure I completely disagree with those statements. If only life was that simple, right? Life is never simple. Life is difficult and complex. I will never agree with anyone who gives such simple explanations and solutions, and then when they don't work out, there is always an excuse.

In a Universe that is always growing, expanding, and changing, you must expect that all elements of the Universe, such as Synchronicities, will also be moving and bending. The Universe is a tricky thing. So are Synchronicities.

Let's now examine some individual topics that are related to Synchronicities. Let me preface by saying my definitions or terms may be different from definitions you have seen in other books or from other Spiritual leaders. I march to my own drumbeat and believe in the information I am given from the higher powers of the Universe. I am not afraid to disagree with other spiritual professionals.

SOUL MATES

I define a Soul Mate as another person who you feel deeply connected with on a soul level. What does "on a soul level" mean? It means you do not just find them sexy, or interesting, or kind, or intellectually stimulating. It is more. You feel as if you already know them or have known them in a past life. You feel an unusual comfort and familiarity with them. There may be a deep trust that is immediate without them having earned it. It feels as if maybe you could be related to them, but you are not.

The test is really about how you feel vs. what you know. Meaning, if you do not know them or do not know much about them, yet you feel totally safe, comfortable, familiar, trusting, and perhaps have strong favorable feelings for them, then they could be a Soul Mate.

The other test is asking if you feel as if you knew them in a different lifetime or dimension. I say this because I believe Soul Mates are often people with Soul Energy that you have encountered before in the Universe. I have two theories on this. The first is that your Soul Energy has indeed had significant substantial contact with their Soul Energy somewhere in the Universe before. Therefore, naturally, you would feel as if you already know them, because you do. The two humans may not have ever met, but your Souls may have already met.

My other theory is that a Soul Mate is another person who has at least one particle of your Soul Energy in them. Remember, due to Soul Splitting, it is possible you have a piece or two of your Universe Soul Energy in other places or other people at the same time. So perhaps when we meet another person who happens to have a piece of our own Soul Energy within them, we totally freak, our ears perk up, and we are totally drawn to this other person because they are indeed part of us. This would explain why we sometimes feel as if we are joined to, or a part of, another person we consider to be a Soul Mate. We feel as one with a Soul Mate. Maybe it is because we share the same Soul Energy with them.

However, another possibility is that different Soul Energies are more highly compatible with certain Soul Energies. Think of it as blood types, except if there were millions of blood types. When our Soul Energy bumps into another person with the same "type," there is an immediate strong connection, as if the Souls of a feather want to flock together.

It is important to mention that a Soul Mate can be anyone. It is not automatically a lover. In fact, it is often not a lover. A Soul Mate can be a friend, teacher, mentor, family member, or yes, a lover or spouse. My point is that a Soul Mate is not about romance. A Soul Mate is purely about the deep soul connection.

A person can have more than one Soul Mate. As I described my theories above, finding a Soul Mate involves the Synchronicity of bumping into another person with your same Soul Energy, or Soul Energy you have met before, or Soul Energy of your exact ideal match type. Therefore, a person may meet many Soul Mates in their life, or not meet any. There is some random luck involved in Synchronicities as I have explained.

So many spiritualists would say this next topic belongs in the chapter about Karma. But I will explain why it is very closely related to Soul Mates.

SOUL CONTRACTS

Soul Contracts are thought to be agreements you enter into before you are born into this lifetime. They are agreements to interact, help, or have some significant impact on other person in this lifetime. Or, vice versa, agreements or obligations others have to you.

Soul Contracts are usually one-way agreements. Here is how to recognize them. First, you may have an overwhelming compulsion or sense of responsibility to help a specific person, even if you have no logical obligation to them. You may not even know them that well. Conversely, you may have another person who seems to be going out of their way to help you, even though you never asked, can never repay them, or don't even particularly want their help.

Soul Contracts often feel involuntary, yet at the same time, there is such a strong compulsion to fulfil them. Soul Contracts could also be described as "Soul Ties." It is a strong compulsion or obligation you feel deep inside on a soul level, even though logically there is no obligation.

What Soul Contracts have in common with Soul Mates, is that there is an unexplainable tie between two souls to interact. How Soul Contracts differ from Soul Mates, is that a Soul Mate is permanent, while a Soul Contract is temporary. A Soul Contract is fulfilled once the obligation has been completed. This is why I think they could also be called "Soul Obligations."

My one caveat is to make sure a Soul Contract is genuine, and not just someone trying to manipulate you or use you. How you know the difference is that a Soul Contract will come from within the person helping, while a manipulation will come from the person being helped.

Why and how are Soul Contracts formed? I believe Soul Contracts, like Soul Mates, are based on "relationships" between Soul Energies while they are within the Universe Energy Collective. I will be discussing Karma in the upcoming chapter, and it could be that Soul Contracts are a way of Soul Energies evening out positive/negative energy outputs between Soul Energies. Or in other words, Soul Contracts are a way of fixing some Karma that was out of balance.

Bear in mind Soul Contracts can also involve mutual growth and learning, and not just "help." But my experience has been that Soul Contracts are mostly one person helping another.

However, I do not want to stray very far from the topic of soul connections right now, so let's move onto our next topic of Twin Flames.

TWIN FLAMES

My definition of a Twin Flame is an ideal lover or mate. Notice I used the word "ideal." I am not talking about a "great" lover or mate. I am talking about "ideal," meaning close to perfect. Very rare. The other element to my definition is that it is romantic in nature.

While a Soul Mate can be anyone, and is based purely on a soul connection, a Twin Flame is a soul connection based on a romantic connection. But it is more than just a romantic connection. It is also the idea of an ideal partner or mate.

So, a Twin Flame is not someone you met last weekend and slept with, and have fallen in love, and you think they are sexy and hot. No.

A Twin Flame is someone who you are so compatible with, that the relationship fits like a glove. It is automatic, easy, strong, comfortable, and wonderful. Very rare.

Most people never find a Twin Flame. Despite this, you will hear every couple in love saying they found their Twin Flame. But no. What they found is someone they are totally into, and in love. That is fine also. Almost all couples and marriages consist of two people who fell in love, love being together, do great together, and want to be together forever. Nothing wrong with that. Live long, prosper, and multiply.

But with Twin Flames, we are talking about that perfect match. I would not suggest to anyone they wait for their perfect match or their Twin Flame. If you do, you might end up a skeleton still waiting. Live your life. But for those who are lucky enough to find a Twin Flame, congratulations, and you know exactly what I am talking about.

Now that we have discussed Soul Mates and Twin Flames, let us ask some questions.

How can I find a Soul Mate or Twin Flame? By using the Hunter Equation, of course. Engage with all four elements of the Hunter Equation and maximize each element to your advantage. Have a clear strong specific Intent of finding a Soul Mate or Twin Flame. You have a better chance of finding them if you are actively looking, know what you are looking for, and truly want to find it. Also, take Action. You will need to actively place yourself in situations where finding what you are looking for is more likely. If you see a potential prospect, you need to *act* by approaching them. Thirdly, use External Forces to your advantage. Whatever situations or places the Universe puts you, or forces you into, use it as an opportunity to actively search for who you are looking for. Lastly, random luck is involved, but realize you have to be in it to win it, and the more you play, the better your chances.

Can someone be my Twin Flame, but I am not their Twin Flame? No! You are either Twin Flames, or you are not. The reason is that part of the definition, is that you both be ideal partners and mates. You cannot be an ideal partner or mate if the other person does not feel the same way.

Can someone be my Soul Mate, but I am not their Soul Mate? Yes. The definition of a Soul Mate is more one sided than the definition of a Twin Flame. Therefore, as long as your Soul Energy recognizes their Soul Energy as a match, then it is a Soul Mate match for you. It could be the other person's Soul Energy does not recognize your Soul Energy as a match because of a difference in perception. For example, let us say your Souls met in a different lifetime. Your Soul became very attached to them and liked them. But perhaps their Soul Energy never really noticed your Soul Energy and did not develop the same feelings. Well then, in the next current life you are in now, their Soul Energy might not really recognize yours, or may not have the same reaction because the prior connection was not as strong for them as it was for you.

What if I find a Soul Mate or Twin Flame, but lose them? Meaning, we never come together in a solid way, or we break up, or we are separated and lose our connection? Well, the problem with Synchronicities is that sometimes things do not fall into sync, and a synchronicity is not formed or completed. Part of the pesky Hunter Equation is that External Forces or Random Luck can screw it all up for us. The Universe is a tricky place. But you can fight back. Use the Hunter Equation to fight back and find them or regain them. Use the four elements to your full advantage to find them, win them over, and get them. Some things are worth searching for, waiting for, and fighting for. Your Intent needs to make those decisions so that your Actions know what to do next.

Some of you might say, "What if I am starting to not like this Hunter Equation stuff, and other Spiritualists have told me that Law of Attraction can get me anything I want, and it's easier." Well, okay, let us talk about that.

LAW OF ATTRACTION

What is The Law of Attraction? Don't quote me. Different people define it slightly different ways. Related to "The Secret," it is a philosophy that says we bring into our life what we think. So, if we have negative thoughts or specific fears, we will end up creating a self-fulfilling prophecy, and those negative things will then come into our lives. Conversely, if we only think positive thoughts with a clear intention of something we want in our lives, then that thing we want will somehow come into our lives.

The Law of Attraction is basically saying we can manifest anything we want based on a clear intention and positive thinking focused on our desired goal. Yeah, there is more to it, but if we are all honest with ourselves, I have summed it up well.

Here is why it does not work. Well first, let me apologize for completely rejecting it out of hand without any fanfare, since millions of people live by it. But firstly, the entire principle is flawed because it violates the Hunter Equation.

Law of Attraction assumes that the Destiny and Free Will are totally valid and are completely determined by Intention and Actions. It thinks the other two elements of External Forces and Random Luck, either do not exist, or are not a factor. It is an inconvenient truth that External Forces and Random Luck *do* exist and *are* a factor.

Sometimes it does not matter how strong of an intention we have, how many actions we take, or how hard we work, sometimes things do not work out the way we desire. Fact of life.

We all know this. Yet, Law of Attraction somehow gives us false hope that we missed something and maybe there is a magic trick that can make the realities of life just go away. The inconvenient reality of life is that External Forces and Random Luck exist. Those two elements alone, are enough to destroy any dreams you have simply based on having a positive attitude, intentions, and focus on what you want to attract.

My gosh, I'm such a bummer and bubble buster, aren't I?

While Law of Attraction is totally false to me, and just a great way to dangle carrots in front of people and make money on their hopes for an easy magic trick, I do think Law of Attraction has some benefit. The benefit is that Law of Attraction has taught people the importance of Intention. Intention, or Intent, is one of my four elements in my equation, and thus very important. If a person has learned how to very effectively create a strong Intent through studying Law of Attraction, then they have helped themselves a great deal. Despair not, all you Law of Attraction people, as you have learned very important lessons and skills when it comes to the element of Intent.

Honestly, I think I have provided enough support to debunk Law of Attraction. But let me add another angle. This is the angle I use often as it makes me very angry about Law of Attraction.

I get very angry when Law of Attraction gurus blame people for their unfortunate outcomes. If you end up in a very poor situation, a Law of Attraction expert would tell you that *you* created your bad situation yourself by your own thoughts and intent. This is narcissistic at its base level. This assumes that all bad things that happen to us are our fault due to our thoughts and intentions.

I raise the question of what about little kids that get cancer? Did the little child have a negative thought and bring cancer into their lives? Is it their fault they have cancer? I think not. What about the soldier who gets his leg blown off by an IED? Did that soldier make that happen to himself by his intentions and negative thoughts? Seriously? Personally, I get offended by such assertions.

However, usually what will happen is that a Law of Attraction person will ignore all the negative things and just focus on the positive outcomes. They will claim victory on the job landed using Law of Attraction, but they will not claim ownership over the kid who got cancer. I'm sorry, but you cannot have it both ways. A Universal principle is either Universal or it is not. It is either a law or it is not. You cannot ignore one side of an equation. We all must be honest with ourselves and look at Truth, even if it is an inconvenient Truth. With all that above said, I could still put a positive spin on the Law of Attraction to give some of you some comfort and solace. Let us just say that the Hunter Equation *builds upon* the Law of Attraction, by simply adding the elements of External Forces, and Random Luck to the equation. So, you can still use the Law of Attraction, so long as you add those last two elements of the Hunter Equation.

How is that? Now let us dry those crocodile tears. It will be okay.

This chapter was kind of brutal because the truth can be brutal. Sometimes Synchronicities can be a wonderful gift. Other times, we miss them, and they do not happen even though we so desperately want them and need them. The bottom line is that Synchronicities do exist, but we do not control them, nor do they appear upon our demand.

Synchronicities, like everything else, are driven by the Hunter Equation and its four elements.

CHAPTER 12

Karma

In Wikipedia, Karma is defined as: it refers to the spiritual principle of cause and effect where intent and actions of an individual (cause) influence the future of that individual (effect). Good intent and good deeds contribute to good karma and future happiness, while bad intent and bad deeds contribute to bad karma and future suffering. Most people would say Karma is reward for good behavior, and punishment for bad behavior. Meaning, if I do bad things, Karma will punish me, but if I do good things, Karma will reward me.

So, what does that mean? Is there some kind of fairy, monster, ghost, God, or troll, that watches us, and if they see us do something bad, they will sneak up on us and punish us? Or is the Karma Master God? Or is Karma some kind of Energy that judges us?

People seem afraid of Karma, in the sense they really believe it exists. Some people will actually say that they do nice things for others, so they can have good Karma. Other people will literally threaten their enemies with bad Karma. So, people do seem convinced Karma is real and exists.

I think we must narrow things down a bit so that we can truly figure out what Karma is, and if it is real. Firstly, can we all agree there is no Karma fairy, monster, ghost, or troll? If we can agree to that, then that means Karma must be from God (the Universe) or some kind of Energy (the Universe). Based on what I just said, we seem to have a winner. Karma is from the Universe (God). So how is it that the Universe is judging our actions and deciding if we deserve good Karma or bad Karma? Or perhaps, what we really need to do is look in the mirror. *We* are part of the Universe, and *We* are doing the good and bad actions. Plus, we seem to be judging the actions as good or bad, so *we* are also the judges. Now it is starting to sound like, *we* the humans, are the Karma fairies handing out good or bad Karma. Could it be that we have been afraid of our own shadows all this time, and that we humans are the ones responsible for Karma? I think we are getting somewhere now, are we not?

But let us take another closer look at the definition of Karma. Karma is a "spiritual principle of cause and effect where **intent** and **actions** of an individual (cause) influence the **future** of that individual (effect). Good intent and good deeds contribute to good karma and future happiness, while bad intent and bad deeds contribute to bad karma and future suffering."

If I am not mistaken, I spot two elements from the Hunter Equation there, plus the other half of the equation, being "future." Again,

Hunter Equation:
Future Outcome = (Intent + Actions + External Forces + Random Luck).

So basically, Karma is stating that a person's future is dependent upon half of the elements from the Hunter Equation. That is it? Is it that simple? Your future is decided on only two of the elements, similar to Law of Attraction? I would say no.

Therefore, right off the bat I would say the Karma definition is flawed, which means the very meaningfulness of Karma is likely flawed. Does this mean Karma is false, fake, and garbage? Absolutely not.

The reason I still think Karma has validity is because it does indeed overlap half of the Hunter Equation. Which makes it half-correct and half-valid. Let us think about it.

If you have bad Intent, and do bad Actions, it is plausible you will end up with a bad future outcome. I cannot disagree with that. Thus, you would indeed "have bad Karma." The reverse is also true when you have good Intent and good Actions. You would then possibly get a good future outcome. My point though, is that these outcomes are not guaranteed. The reason why is because the other two elements, External Forces and Random Luck, can still throw off your results.

This explains why some people do not understand why Karma did not reward them, or why Karma did not punish someone else. For example, if someone has the bad Intent and Actions of stealing candy from a baby, they should in theory, receive bad Karma. But sometimes they do not. Sometimes they can steal candy from a baby and still lead a successful happy life filled with wonderful things. Why is this? It is because they may have had External Forces step in and thrust them to great fortune, along with Random Luck stepping in and also giving them great luck and fortune. In this example, everyone thought the person deserved bad Karma, but they never received bad Karma because the other two elements of the Hunter Equation saved them.

Conversely, many people complain how they do good deeds every day, but still have bad Karma. True, they may have had good Intent and good Actions, but if the External Forces and Random Luck were running against them, then they may have had a bad Future Outcome.

With all that said, we have already talked about how your best chances of a good outcome is to maximize all four elements in your favor. This would mean having good Intent and good Actions. In this way, Karma as most think of it, is still relevant.

Let me give one more example of how the flawed concept of Karma is still relevant and needs to be considered. Karma is an excellent measuring device for the output of positive and negative energy. Let us go through a real-life scenario to examine this concept.

Let us say we have a very mean boss who is going to fire an employee simply because he does not like them. Maybe the employee likes an opposing sports team, or is of a different skin color, or of a sexual orientation the boss does not approve, or is of an opposing political affiliation, or just in some way annoys the boss. So, the boss fires the employee. For this example, we will say the Action by the boss has resulted in 100 units of negative energy.

That negative energy the boss just released into the Universe has to get absorbed. It will get absorbed by the employee who just lost their job. The employee will feel sad, angry, depressed, and scared. The negative energy will be absorbed by the employee's family. The employee's spouse will be sad, angry, and scared. The employee's children might be frightened. Thus, the negative energy is absorbed by them also. The wave of negative energy might continue on to the employee's parents who are then asked for financial help or are concerned. The employee might have trouble paying their car payment and rent, so the negative energy is also absorbed by the landlord and car finance company. You get the point.

That 100 units of negative energy hits many people and is absorbed by all those people. That one Action, resulting in the release of 100 units of negative energy, has now affected many people in a spreading domino effect, and has been absorbed by all those people.

Some would say that is some pretty nasty Karma that should be coming back to the mean boss. The question is, will the boss eventually be hit with 100 units of negative energy in return, as a result of his bad Action of firing the employee for illegitimate reasons? Well, we discussed above, it may or may not. Certainly, other employees will have seen what he did and perhaps look for a new job out of fear they will be unfairly fired as well. That would result in hitting the mean boss with some units of negative energy, but certainly not the full 100 units.

As stated above, it is hard to say if the boss will receive bad Karma or not. It depends on all the elements of the Hunter Equation. But let's make this more interesting for a moment. Pretend the boss wakes up in the middle of the night and realizes he was wrong and now he feels bad. Perhaps he fears bad Karma coming his way. How can the boss right this wrong and relieve his selfish fear of bad Karma coming his way?

I have seen humans approach this a few different ways. One way, is they go to the person they have wronged and apologize, hoping it all goes away. Would an apology to the employee fix the situation? No. The problem is that 100 units of negative energy was released, and it was absorbed by many different people. The boss would have to apologize to the spouse, children, parents, car finance company, landlord, and so on. Even then, simple words might not be enough to offset 100 units of negative energy.

I have seen other humans simply go to their place of worship and ask God for forgiveness. If they can leave their place of worship feeling they were forgiven, or their religious leader says they are forgiven, does that mean all is okay again? Well, were the 100 units of negative energy absorbed by all those people offset by this visit to the place of worship and talking to God? Umm, no.

Really, the only way to fix a situation like this is if the boss finds a way to offset the 100 units of negative energy. To do this, he might need to release 100 units or more of positive energy. In other words, some "Action" will be required to release positive energy to offset the negative energy. OR, the boss could go to those people damaged and offset the negative energy by taking it back upon himself. He could do this by paying the late rent due, paying the late car payment, making the children happy instead of scared, and so on and so forth. It is a lot of work to fix the 100 units of damage the boss did. But it could be done.

So, the above scenario is an example of how people see Karma, and how it can float around and boomerang back, or not. More importantly, it is an example of how bad deeds, or bad karma, cannot be fixed by simple thoughts or gestures. There must be real Actions, to match unit for unit, in order to fix it.

In summary, Karma on its surface has some validity. But Karma as a literal definition, principle, and law, is flawed, and cannot function as it is expected. Therefore, Karma is only real if you do not take it too literally.

Additionally, any Karmic rewards or punishments are clearly being dealt by other humans, including yourself.

It is an important footnote to point out that some religious beliefs, such as Buddhism, consider Karma an important part of their belief system. Why is this? I believe, like most religious beliefs, certain principles are used in order to create a moral boundary of behavior. If a belief system says you need to treat others well in order to have good Karma, well who am I to protest? I am in favor of good Intents and good Actions.

If a religious belief wants to promote Karma as important, so that people feel they must treat others well, then I think it is wonderful. I have nothing against it. My goal in this book is not to throw shade on everyone's religious beliefs, or otherwise. My goal is to illuminate Truth as it has been shown to me. Usually the Truth is in the middle. Karma is an excellent example of a principle that is kind of true, but not to the full extent some say.

I would urge everyone, and all religious beliefs, to continue considering Karma as a valuable moral compass, because it is.

CHAPTER 13

How Are Psychics Psychic?

There is much legend and misperception surrounding psychic abilities. Some psychics might say they are super powers given to the worthy and the lucky. Some people think psychic abilities are some kind of clever magic trickery. Some religions view psychics as evil scary people using powers that only God is allowed to use.

People always fear what they do not understand, and anything not fully understood is usually surrounded by conspiracy and suspicion. Since some things are not yet scientifically proven, it allows people to make up anything and say anything they want about it. People once thought the world was flat.

I could probably write an entire book on psychic abilities and being psychic. So, what I am going to do here, just like most topics in this book, is that I am going to give you the cliff notes version, so you can better understand what psychic abilities are, and how some people are psychic.

Psychic abilities are not magic. They are also not super powers. Psychic abilities are more similar to a dog whistle. They are something that intrinsically exist already, but only some people can "hear them". Just like how a dog whistle is there, but only dogs can hear it. Similar to a dog whistle, psychic abilities are there for everyone, but not everyone can engage them.

Again, since I am not writing an entire book on this, and just doing one chapter, I am going to simplify things. Therefore, I ask my psychic friends to please refrain from sending me hate mail on how I over simplified things and did not cover all the various complexities.

Being a psychic is the same as being a radio. A psychic has the ability to tune into many various frequencies. The Universe is the radio stations. The Universe sends out energy in the form of pulse waves. These energy waves carry specific frequencies. A psychic is able to detect these incoming energy waves and tune into the specific frequencies, to "hear" the information.

First, let us talk more about these energy waves from the Universe. They are not necessarily powerful fast-moving waves sent from far away galaxies. Many of these waves are emitted very short distances, or even somewhat static.

Let me give you an example of a more static energy wave. If someone was brutally murdered in a room, there would have been a huge discharge of energy from the event. That energy discharge would have gone into the room, the walls, the furniture, and so on. If a psychic walks into that room, a psychic can sense that energy. The energy is stored in the walls of the room, the objects, and the air. So, the energy waves are not traveling distances. The energy is mostly static in the room. The energy is emanating only a few feet or inches from the walls and objects. Sometimes a psychic needs to actually touch the walls or objects to feel the energy, thus the energy waves are not traveling any distance, except from the object to the psychic's hand. This is an example of energy waves that are effectively static, but the psychic has tuned into the frequency and can hear it.

But in many cases, the energy waves travel significant distances and the psychic must tune into the correct frequency carefully to hear the information. For example, if a psychic is sitting at their desk and their client asks them a question about a future outcome, the psychic must determine the correct frequency to tune into, and then effectively tune into that frequency and listen for the information. The frequency from those energy waves are likely coming from some Universal source, such as the Akashic records, or another person the client is engaging with. The psychic must decide the most effective way to get the answer the client is looking for. The psychic may decide to tune into another living person associated with the client. In this case, the psychic will tune into that frequency of that other person, even if the other person is thousands of miles away.

Everything in the Universe gives off these energy waves with frequencies. The entire Universe consists of energy as we have previously discussed. Energy is everywhere. Any psychic can tell you how "noisy" the world is. That is why some psychics become overwhelmed by the "noise" and need to find a way to "switch off." Basically, the energy of the information is not the problem. The challenge is more in effectively tuning into the energy the best most efficient ways.

A client may also ask a psychic to tune into the energy of a deceased loved one. This is called Mediumship. Psychic Mediums specialize in communicating with the dead. In this case, the psychic specifically tunes into the frequency of energy coming from the deceased person's soul energy. Since a person's soul consists of Universal Energy, that energy gives off energy waves. A psychic can effectively tune into that specific frequency, and that specific energy, in order to hear the information. A very skilled psychic can lock onto that energy and have a back and forth communication with that energy. Thus, a psychic can communicate with the dead.

Communicating with the dead sounds so magical and scary. But really, it is just a matter of tuning into the correct frequency for that soul energy of that specific person and being able to listen and hear what the energy is saying. I feel like I am taking away the magic for some of you, or telling you the Easter Bunny is not real, but the point of this book is to unveil the mysteries of the Universe, right? By the way, the Easter Bunny IS real, for any young people reading this. But I will not cover it further in this book.

Let's look at another angle. A client will often ask the psychic what is in their future. How can a psychic see the future? Well, in my personal opinion, a psychic does not specifically see the future. The reason being that the future is not written in stone. But, before you all yell at me, a psychic sees something very similar to the future. A psychic is able to tune into all the frequencies surrounding a person, hear, read, and interpret those energy waves, and then calculate the most likely future.

In other words, a psychic can tune into the energy, read all the energy, and then calculate the trajectory of all that energy. The psychic can view the trajectory of the energy and where all the actions are heading, and with high accuracy predict what will happen in the future. The complicated part of this is the psychic is often tuning into a huge multitude of sources to gain their information.

For example, if a person asks me if they will get a job they are applying for, I would have to tune into many different energy sources. I would tune into the client, the prospective employer, the employer's industry, the employer's customers, the location of employment, Universal sources such as the Akashic records, and so on and so forth. I would draw from many different energy sources before I would come up with my "read" on what I think will happen or what I "see" happening in the future.

Not to burst any bubbles, but I do not believe in looking into a crystal ball and seeing a movie of what will happen. I believe in tuning into a multitude of real actual Universal energies and reading that energy the best I can. By the way, I *have* looked into crystal balls before, and I've seen things and it is fun. But like reading palms, it is kind of for entertainment only. So, have fun. Do it. But when it's time to get serious, you need a psychic who tunes into the frequencies of all the Universal energies to accurately compute the most likely future outcome.

With all that said above, I should point out that many psychics, me included, *do* see images or short movies of the future. But it is still based upon our calculations of the most likely outcomes. The final outcome cannot be seen, because there are too many variables that can change the Future Outcome, such as uncalculated random events.

Another major source of psychic ability is by tuning into a psychic's "Guides," or "Spirit Guides." "Guides" are actual entities, most of which could have been living humans at some point. As we already discussed, a psychic can tune into the soul energy of a deceased person. A "Spirit Guide" or "Guide," is an entity, or deceased person, which the psychic has *locked* onto their energy. So, the energy of this entity is always with the psychic and easily tuned into. Since the psychic does not have to spend much time or effort finding the right frequency or tuning into that energy, the psychic can very easily and quickly tap into that energy of the Guide. The psychic can then ask that energy questions and listen for an answer. It is very similar to doing psychic medium work with the dead. However, with guides, the energy follows the psychic wherever they go and is always present.

Very often, I am asked to tune into a client's Guides and describe to the client who their Guides are. Since everything is energy, and their Guides emit energy, I can tune into that energy and often describe what I am hearing, seeing, and picking up on. The Guide often turns out to be some deceased loved one, ancestor, or someone the client has always resonated with.

Much of what I have discussed above is about the Universal energy going outward, and how it is transmitted to the psychic. I would be remiss if I did not briefly go into more detail about the psychic or "radio" end of things. Like a good radio or TV, a good psychic is able to clearly tune into the correct signal using all possible methods.

A psychic can often see, hear, and feel the energy. A psychic, tunes into the correct frequency, then listens to the energy on all levels in order to gain the most accurate "read" of the energy. So, when I am doing a reading and tuning into the energies, I am opening myself up to seeing anything that comes into my mind, hearing anything that comes into my mind, and feeling or sensing anything that comes into my mind, heart, and soul. I am opening up all my senses to the frequency, and hoping some information is received.

I also want to cover a more advanced psychic skill. Have you ever wondered how a psychic can do "energy work?" Energy work is when a psychic is able to influence, manipulate, or control energy in the client's favor. A couple examples might be when a psychic healer is able to somehow perform healing work from a distance. Or when a psychic is seemingly able to influence an outcome for you, such as you meeting a new person? Is this all for real? How does it work?

Like any profession, anyone can claim to be able to do anything even if they cannot. So, there are some psychics who try to dupe clients into paying for such energy work when they cannot deliver results.

However, a talented skilled psychic *can* influence and manipulate energy for the purposes of healing or providing a desired outcome. I could write an entire book explaining the complexities and details of how this is done. But let me give you a brief explanation.

Basically, a psychic can manipulate energy by using a few tools all at the same time. First, remember the Hunter Equation is always in play and one of the elements is External Forces. A skilled psychic is able to influence the External Forces. How do they do this?

Psychics can push upon the External forces by asking Spirit Guides to provide an External Force, or by pushing upon the Energy waves themselves. Some psychics can impact and move Energy by thought. Energy consists of various waves and particles, and these can be moved like anything else. Healing is often performed by speeding up certain energy around the injury, such as spinning energy at a high speed around a wound, which then speeds up recovery. I was actually taught how to do this in a tiny old empty church in England once, by an entity who appeared as light. But I digress.

The point is that energy is essentially a substance that can be touched, moved, and manipulated. I can do energy work for the client's benefit by gaining some control over the energy, and then using the Hunter Equation on it. I would plug in the client's desired Future Outcome, then I would impact upon the energy using a very strong Intent, asking it, and pushing it, toward Actions. I would then hope those Actions result in some External Forces, which push a situation more in the client's favor. I would also ask Spirit Guides to influence the situation by pushing on the External Forces in the client's favor. It is all very mechanical and scientific in a way. It is also exhausting. The energy output required is huge. Nothing in this Universe is free, and if you expect a large energy income of benefit, you need to expect a large output of energy to create it. But really, it is all quite logical, and depends upon developing certain skills, and knowing how to apply those skills.

Maybe you are seeing by now why I am saying that being psychic is not about magic. Being psychic is about training your mind, body, and soul to completely open up to all Universal energy waves coming in from specific certain frequencies you want to tune into. It is a skill actually. Yes, to hear a dog whistle, you need to have the ability to pick up on frequencies and energy that most cannot sense. But it is also about having the skills to listen for the right whistles and pitches, and knowing which whistle is the one to listen to.

Being psychic is something that most everyone can develop in my opinion. The only difference is that for some of us, it was natural and very strong. For others, it may need lots of work to bring it out and develop. But all the energy, frequencies, and information, is already intrinsically there. All that is required is the skill and ability to effectively tune into it and read it.

That bad news is that there is no mystery here. No magic. No super powers. The good news is that it is real and scientifically based, even if science has not caught up to it yet.

CHAPTER 14

Angels, Ghosts & Demons

We cannot talk about the Universe without talking about paranormal entities. Like many topics within this book, different people will have different definitions and opinions of what things are.

I am sharing my own personal ideas and definitions, many of which align very nicely with what others think. However, as you have seen, I have my own specific ideas of how things might work. That is no different when it comes to paranormal entities.

ANGELS

Most think of Angels as heavenly spirits or entities who are benevolent in nature and have the power of God's hand to intervene in human lives for the benefit of individuals or humanity.

Angels are seen as having the ability to directly help people, provide comfort, or even manifest miracles. So, what are they really? Do they fly around with their wings answering people's prayers and wishes all day? Are they servants of God?

Well here is what I think. Firstly, there are different types of angels. Let us talk about Living Angels. Living Angels are real people currently alive, who are by all accounts, doing God's work. Meaning, these people spend the majority of their time, effort, and resources, helping other people. The most famous would be Mother Teresa while she was alive. But there are many more who never see fame or any attention for their deeds. Earth Angels come in all shapes and sizes. I have found most to be very modest people with little money, who still do extraordinary things for other people. They likely have a tremendous amount of empathy and put other people ahead of themselves. They always seem to be there to step into someone's life when the person needs it most. They give and help without condition. They seemingly have completely given themselves to the service of others without any guarantee of reward. When you ask them about what they do, they often say, "It's my calling," "It's the right thing to do." They are benevolent, caring, giving, generous, and are happy to do so without any recognition or great reward. I love these people.

Now to the Angels who are not living humans. Guardian Angels are Angels whose specific job is to be the last line of defence in protection. Guardian Angels are very often Spirit Guides who take on double duty. I will talk about Spirit Guides in a bit. Guardian Angels are often specific to certain people. Thus, they have some soul tie or soul connection to that specific human. Guardian Angels often rush in and provide miracles to facilitate the safety or survival of humans in trouble. We are always grateful for their presence.

Next, we examine more closely what we think of as traditional Angels, most of which we may have no personal connection. As I established, the Universe Energy Collective is full of Soul Energy. I believe Ghosts among these soul energy entities are those souls who have chosen to remain in the Universal Energy Collective, rather than be fully reincarnated. These souls remain in a soul energy state and thus have the powers and abilities of all the energy that remains in the Collective. They have access to the Akashic records of knowledge, they can travel at instantaneous speeds, and they are in full connection with all Universal Energy such that they always know everything that is going on at all times in all places.

I believe they are souls, or soul energy, who are no longer on a soul journey of reincarnating and living organic lives, but rather are devoting themselves to the service of the Universe as a whole, which includes humanity. So again, they are truly selfless and giving in nature, even when in soul energy form. They likely intervene under certain Universal laws. This is why direct contact with Angels is rare, and Angels often only help, rather than provide full solutions. Angels help people; they do not do everything for people. When you call upon an Angel, you can expect benevolent responses, but usually only partial help or solution. Most of the heavy lifting is always the responsibility of the human. Anyone asking Angels to solve all their problems for them will be disappointed. But the good news is that this benevolent intelligent soul energy is indeed available to us and we should be very grateful for their service to the Universe.

What are Archangels? Without getting into a long religious discussion, it is thought there are seven angels of God. They are called archangels. Archangel Michael and Archangel Gabriel would be the most famous I suppose. Religious texts would have various stories of why each of the archangels are heroes of God. I am including them in our discussion because so many people hear about, talk about them, and pray to these archangels. It is really not that crazy, and I believe in the concept. Here is why.

Let's step back for a moment and remember what I consider God to be. I believe God is real, and God exists, in the form of the Universe. The Universe consists of all this living intelligent Universal Energy, which is soul energy. All this living soul energy in the Collective is "the light." It *is* God.

Archangels are thought to be heroes of God. They are thought to be very powerful Angels that humans can call upon for help. Well I believe that to be true. As God is the Universe, I believe the Archangels are symbols of the benevolent Soul Energy that exists to serve the Universe, and thus humanity. An Archangel is the "face" we put to this soul energy, just as God is the "face" we put to the Universe. Having archangels with specific names help us humanize this soul energy of the Universe which actually exists and helps us.

I am even willing to go so far as to say there are different energy signatures for different soul energies, and thus this makes the soul energy seem like "individuals", which can be separated into different archangels.

So as God exists, so do Archangels. The Universe is what it is, and truth is truth. But we all have the freedom to view the Universe through whatever prism we choose. I think Archangels is a totally valid and good way to view the benevolent soul energy within the Universe Energy Collective.

SPIRIT GUIDES

Spirit Guides are souls, or soul energy, which are specific to you and each human. They often consist of loved ones or relatives who have passed, or those with some kind of soul connection to you. Spirit Guides often serve very specific purposes. For example, you might have one Spirit Guide who helps you make decisions, and another Spirit Guide who provides you comfort during rough emotional times. I personally have numerous Spirit Guides who provide me with expertise in certain areas when needed. Often there is a primary Spirit Guide who looks over us and acts as our primary support.

A person can be taught to communicate with their Spirit Guide, just as psychics can often sense and describe your Spirit Guide for you. Spirit Guides are wonderful blessings of soul energy that always remain close to us that we can draw upon as needed.

GHOSTS

Ghosts are essentially energy that is "Earth bound," or still here with us on the ground, as opposed to back in the Universe Energy Collective. However, Ghosts come in different forms.

An active Ghost, or what I might call a "Living Ghost," is actual soul energy of a person that has not left the ground. This is the type of ghost that most people are afraid of, because it still is capable of moving about with free will. The soul energy for one reason or another did not go up to the Universe Energy Collective. It did not go up to the light, or back to God, so to speak.

The reasons may vary. Perhaps the soul energy got confused, trapped, or is held on Earth by some unresolved issue. Perhaps it is only still on Earth temporarily. But for whatever reason, the soul energy is still here.

Since the energy is so strong with this type of Ghost, the Ghost can often be seen with the human eye, as vapor of some sort. This type of ghost can also be communicated with if it wishes to cooperate.

Another type of Ghost is what I call "Static Remnant Energy." It is really not a ghost at all, but since it feels like a ghost, I call it a ghost. This is energy that has been left behind by an event. Let's say a person died in a room. Some of the energy that was released during the death process, may be imbedded into the air, walls, floor, or ceiling of the room. This energy may be strong enough to emit a ghostly feel to it. People will think it is a ghost. But really, it is leftover energy that is just sitting there. So, it is not an active living ghost per se. But it is still ghostly and creepy.

Ghosts can also come and go, flash in and flash out. I consider these ghosts to be the troublemakers. These ghosts are fully capable of going to the light up to the Universe Energy Collective, but for some reason choose to still "haunt" the ground. They have unresolved issues, or just like causing mayhem. They usually cannot be seen with the human eye. But can be felt and detected.

POLTERGEIST

A Poltergeist is a concentration of ghost energy, soul energy, or Universe Energy, which is strong enough to have direct contact with this dimension of the living. Meaning, this energy is able to move objects, touch things, and make noises. This is obviously terrifying to most people. Poltergeists can be from active ghosts, flash in and out ghosts, or Demons, which we will talk about next. A lot more research needs to be done on Poltergeists, as they seem capable of things that are logically impossible. But to me, it is completely logical in the sense that enough energy highly concentrated, could certainly be expected to move objects.

DEMONS

Demons are considered to be those paranormal entities which are malevolent or evil in intent. So, a Demon may be a Ghost, Poltergeist, or a collection of energy from the Universe, but is meant to cause harm.

Demons are possibly the most feared entity by humans. They are not understood, usually given very scary appearances, very difficult to get rid of, and capable of stirring the darkest scariest hysteria.

Where there is light, there is dark. Where there is good, there is bad. There is much light in the Universe. I have spent this entire book talking about the light pretty much. But there is also darkness. A Demon would consist of dark energy. This is energy that has negative intent. Energy may contain negative intent for various reasons. I think of it as hundreds of water faucets giving the life of water to everyone, but then what wastewater goes down the drain, empties into the sewer system, and comes out in one awful sewer pipe, full of the dirtiest most awful substance; that would be your dark energy. The dark dirty energy exists somewhere. Where did you think it went? It exists in the form of Demons.

To be honest, I have rarely come into contact with genuine Demons. I have dealt with many living humans who I felt were just as bad as Demons, but no actual paranormal Demons, except a couple times. So, for me at least, Demons are rare. But they exist.

Demons feed on fear and live in the form of hate. Feeling fear only feeds the Demon and makes it more capable of harm. Its energy output is in the form of hate. So, it is fear going in, and hate coming out. It is important to remember this, so the next time you are dealing with a Demon you know how to disarm it.

Actually, do not mess with Demons. Call someone. Ghost Busters maybe. Or me!

CHAPTER 15

Divine Intervention

Wikipedia defines Divine Intervention as a purported miracle caused by a deity's active involvement in the human world. Let us examine that. So, it is a miracle caused by a deity's active involvement in the human world. What I would rephrase that to, is: Divine Intervention is a miracle (desired outcome) caused by God's (The Universe's) active involvement in the human world. Or we can say, Divine Intervention is a desired Future Outcome caused by the Action of the Universe Energy, as an External Force toward humans.

Divine Intervention is sounding like a very Hunter Equation kind of event. The definition itself essentially contains multiple elements of the Hunter Equation.

Yes, some people are probably doing an eye roll and saying I have just complicated it. Most think of Divine Intervention as God stepping in to help us. But that is exactly what I am saying. God (The Universe), does step in (take Actions) to help us (External Force), to create miracles (desired Future Outcomes).

So, the good news is that I am totally on board with this Divine Intervention stuff. It passes the smell test from a Theologian point of view, as well as a Hunter Equation point of view. It is as if it is scientific and logical, in addition to being, a major pillar of religious and spiritual faith. Don't you just love it when all kinds of contrarian lines cross and overlap, and it just confirms that something *has* to be true!

Therefore, I am a total believer in Divine Intervention. Just like humans have the ability to have Intent and take Action, so does the intelligent Energy of the Universe. It is quite similar to how non-human Angelic beings have the ability to create Action and Intent that results in an External Force that affects humans in a benevolent way.

Why does Divine Intervention happen? I believe there are two possible answers for this. First, some energy in the Universe decides to make it happen. Secondly, humans decide to make it happen. Let me explain further.

Energy in the Universe is intelligent, especially entities such as Angels and Spirit Guides. Angels and Spirit Guides specifically, exist to provide support for souls existing in human form. Our Spirit Guides and Angels are there to help us and protect us. It is only logical that in the normal course of them doing so, they would proactively initiate Actions to provide External Forces which will result in giving us some positive result or outcome that we so desperately need. We humans would interpret such an act as a miracle coming from the heavens, which is exactly what it is. For some reason, these entities from the Universe intelligently determined or intended that we humans needed the assistance. So, they assisted in their own way.

The other way Divine Intervention can occur is through the initiation of a human. A person asks for help or asks for this miracle. This is most commonly referred to as "prayer." A human prays for a certain Future Outcome.

Who or what do they pray to? They pray to God (the Universe), or even specifically to the Angels or their Spirit Guides. What is prayer? Prayer is a very strong intense specific request for a Future Outcome. The prayer is almost always given with a very strong Intent.

I hate to do this to you again, but basically, when someone prays, they are using the Hunter Equation because they are requesting a Future Outcome using very strong Intent, and hoping the Universe takes an Action that creates an External Force, that gives them what they are requesting. Since none of this can be proven and it is all invisible, it can also feel to the human like Random Luck is involved. Thus, all elements of the Hunter Equation are engaged.

Therefore, I am also a total believer in the power of prayer. Here is the only caveat. Usually when I talk about taking Actions within the Hunter Equation, I am referring to Actions that you personally need to take yourself. People are responsible for themselves and their own Actions and need to take control and responsibility over their own life equation. But sometimes when things are desperate, we are tired, and we need help, it's okay to ask for help. Prayer is that way of asking for help.

So how can I make my prayer as effective as possible? Simply apply the Hunter Equation to your prayers. Meaning, be mindful to make your Future Outcome specific and righteous. Do not ask for something meaningless or out of greed. Then pray with deep Intent. Furthermore, to help your prayer along, think of any Actions you personally can take which may assist in the success of the Future Outcome you are praying for. Finally, clear the way of any External Force obstructions you can clearly see coming, but also be open to the fact that your prayer may be answered through an unexpected External Force.

For example, if you pray for a pony, do not expect a pony to show up on your doorstep. What might happen is you find out that a friend of a friend had a friend who was taking care of a pony, but had to move, and they need someone to take over the pony. This would be a weird External Factor coming at you, which is actually the result of your prayer. You need to be awake and savvy enough to recognize it when you see it and take advantage of it.

When we pray, we are giving up control over the equation, so that means the Future Outcome might be provided in a weird way we would have never expected or chosen. So be ready to see it, and be ready to accept it, even if you do not think the circumstances are ideal. You gave up your control over the circumstances the moment you gave it over to prayer, instead of your direct Hunter Equation control of Actions.

Know that there is intelligent Universe Soul Energy up there, and here, in the Universe, that is willing and capable to help us by causing External Forces that might be in our favor. All you have to do is ask through prayer. All you prayer warriors, can now make your prayers even more powerful by applying the Hunter Equation to your prayer process.

CHAPTER 16

The Human Experience

So far we have spent a lot of time looking at the Universe and its contents. Now it is time to focus more closely on humans.

Let me preface this chapter by saying I will be taking many liberties in defining things how I personally see them, taken from how they have been described to me by higher powers in the Universe. I will also be looking at things from the perspective of the Universe, rather than a fellow human on the ground. I am looking at things as if I was an alien or a being from the outer Universe. But obviously all of that will be mixed with the fact that I have inside knowledge and experience as a human on Earth.

So, with that said, a Human is a Homo Sapiens. A person. An Earthling. An organic living being, such as animals that roam the Earth, but far more advanced in its cognitive thinking. I think we all know what a human is.

What I really aim to discuss is what a human is, in comparison to other beings. In other words, what makes humans special and unique? What is it like to be human? What does it mean to be human? What is the human experience?

In my opinion, what makes humans special from other creatures and beings in the Universe, is the capacity to experience intense sensations and emotions. I am willing to bet that humans are among the most emotional creatures out there. Emotions and Sensations are very intense for humans.

Thus, experiencing sensations and emotions is the definition of The Human Experience.

Therefore, the more sensations and emotions you experience, the more human you are. We talked before about how your Soul is hoping to have amazing experiences and adventures in its various lives. These human lives add to the Soul's overall depth of existence, growth, and evolution. When a Soul lives a human life, it is no doubt in search of sensations and emotions. It is like when you go into a pizza shop, and most people will order a pizza instead of a salad. You can order a salad if you insist, but the full experience of being in a great pizza shop is ordering a great pizza. So, it would be the same for Souls who inhabit a human for its latest life experience. To gain the fullest experience as a human, the Soul would want to experience as many sensations and emotions as possible. It is the essence of life. To experience sensations and emotions, is to live. Let us look at that.

We will talk about Sensations and Senses first. Some popular human sensations are Touch, Taste, Sight, Smell, and Hearing. You all know those. But I want to add a few more to the conversation. Let us add Pleasure, Pain, and Sex. Those three are also emotion based, but they are key human sensations as well.

Touching something as a human is amazing. Our fingers are so sensitive and can pick up tons of information by touching something. Touching things like Jello, cool water, chalkboards, and other humans, can give us amazing experiences just in themselves. Everyone can think of their favorite things to touch.

Taste is one of my favorites. Humans must eat to survive, just like animals and probably many creatures of the Universe. Humans need fuel for life. But for a human, taking in food, fuel, and sustenance, is not just a necessary chore. It is actually one of the most pleasurable things a human does on a daily basis. The sense of Taste gives us various sensations that can barely be described by words. You know a sensation is special when it cannot be described by words. Therefore, Taste ranks right up there. It certainly has to be one of the greatest most unique sensations and experiences in the Universe; and humans are among the lucky ones to have this.

Sight is pretty obvious. It is also fairly necessary. However, plenty of blind people get through life just fine without sight, by using their other senses. Sight is special because through sight a person can take in more bits of data in a shorter time than any other sense. A picture is worth a thousand words. If you want to convey the most amount of information to someone in the shortest amount of time, you would want to use Sight as your vehicle for that. Our ability to see things is amazing. Our sight is not very good as far as optimal functionality though. Most animals have far better sight than humans do, and thus I am sure plenty of Universal beings do as well. However, sight for humans is not just about functionality. It's about a human's ability to see beauty in sight, and thus experience pleasure, just by using Sight. Pretty extraordinary really.

Smell is an interesting sense because it gives us one of the most diverse human reactions when we experience Smell. Smell can put us in heaven or put us in hell. Smell is a very love or hate sensation. Everyone has their favorite smells, but also smells which can evoke the most repulsive reactions. A human can literally become sick just by the smell of something. That is amazingly powerful.

Hearing is similar to Sight in that it is very necessary to functionality. However, plenty of deaf people do fine in life without hearing. Aside from its obvious functionality of communication, safety, and efficiency, it can also provide us with pleasure. Only behind communication, music would be the next most important experience with the sense of Hearing. Listening to music and enjoying music is probably one of the most epic and popular of all human experiences.

Now for the sensations I added, starting with Pleasure. The Sensation of Pleasure is related to all the senses and Sensations mentioned above. But Pleasure is so important and so key to the human experience that I wanted to mention it separately. Pleasure may very well be one of the reasons we live and endure. Without Pleasure, why bother? Pleasure is *that* important. Pleasure is our incentive for living. We endure all experiences in hopes of experiencing Pleasure, even if fleeting. Once a human dies, I suspect the sensation they miss the most is Pleasure. So that is pretty significant, don't you think?

The equal opposite to Pleasure is Pain. No human wants to experience Pain. However, Pain is very necessary because without Pain, we would not fully appreciate Pleasure. In addition to that, Pain is our most effective safety warning system. When we feel Pain, we immediately know something is wrong, and we take immediate corrective action. This applies to physical pain and mental pain. I would argue that Pain is actually necessary for life, more so than the others. Without Pain, we would surely do stupid things and die early.

Then of course, there is Sex. I may be touching the third rail by saying this, but how can you possibly have a human experience without experiencing Sex. I hope I am not making any virgins out there feel uncomfortable or inadequate, but I have to keep it real.

Sex as a human can be amazing. It can also be horrible if a person has had a horrible experience with sex, such as rape or abuse. But Sex is likely the most intense Sensation of them all. Sex is a sensation that absolutely cannot be described in words. People do not even try to describe it in words. So, without a doubt that makes it epic and amazing. The sensation of Sex, the desire, the yearning, the connection, and the orgasm, are all so intense, that humans are literally shaking and barely keeping themselves together, during and after the experience. I venture to say this sensation is more powerful and intense for humans than most other creatures of the Universe.

After looking at all those senses and sensations, we can see how the human experience is packed with amazing things. All of those make life worth living, and make Souls want to live a life as a human. If that is not enough, we also have all our human Emotions. Emotions in humans are even stronger, more intense, and deeper, than our senses and sensations. Our human Emotions make our senses and sensations seem shallow and simple in comparison.

Emotions are hard to list because there are many, including some not fully defined yet. Also, emotions come in many different shades and moods. But we will cover a few of them. Some common Emotions include Happiness, Sadness, Excitement, Pride, Love, Hate, Anger, Fear, and Greed.

Happiness, or Joy, is a wonderful Emotion. It really cannot be explained in words. It is something that must be experienced to be understood. Imagine life with no Happiness ever experienced. Notice I said, "ever experienced." I totally understand there are some humans who experience very little happiness. But at some point, in every Soul's human experience, some level of Happiness is felt and experienced.

The flip side is of course Sadness. Happiness would have little meaning without also experiencing Sadness. Sadness is a cruel emotion. There really is not anything good about it, except for the fact it is necessary to experience so that we more fully appreciate Happiness.

Excitement, or Anticipation, are very fun human emotions to experience. Most of us have fond memories of experiencing these emotions as a child.

Excitement is certainly more powerful as a child. As we grow older, we intentionally make the emotion of Excitement duller, in order to avoid the emotion of Disappointment. Certainly, Excitement is a very fleeting emotion that we push to the side as we get older, and even when we experience it, the emotion often only lasts for some minutes before fading off. But it was well worth mentioning.

Pride is not often mentioned, except sometimes as a negative or bad thing. But I feel Pride is worth mentioning as a positive emotion worth

112

experiencing. Humans are feeble creatures who often struggle and suffer much. Pride is our reward to enduring the struggles and troubles. The feeling of Pride is a great reward and is something we all strive for, even if some of us will not admit to it for religious, cultural, or other reasons.

Perhaps Love should have been mentioned first or last. Love is the most important human emotion. Love is the most important Universal emotion. Love is the language of the Universe and the language of God. Love is everything. It is the sun that makes us live. Without Love, there is no life really. If there is life, it is empty without Love. We know what Love is. My point here is just to remind everyone of its central importance to humans and the Universe. Love is indescribable. But Love is the deepest of all emotions. True love is eternal.

The opposite of Love is Hate. However, Hate is weak and fleeting. Hate is run by impulse. Hate is also far from eternal. Hate is often very fleeting, although it can last a long time in limited circumstances. Hate is the same as Hurt. Hate is Pain. Hate is the symbol of Pain. Hate is not a worthy human emotion to experience, but Hate, similar to Pain, is a great reminder and warning that something is wrong. Hate is an affliction and an illness.

Anger is a very common emotion that causes us the most problems. Anger is usually fleeting. However, Anger is most likely to cause us to do stupid things we later regret. Anger is one of the most intense emotions a human can experience. Anger is unusual because even though it is so intense, it is very shallow at the same time. Some humans can have a deep anger for a long time, but those humans really are classified as mentally ill or damaged on some level. Nobody should experience Anger for more than short moments. If you feel Anger for long periods of time, you should seek help or something bad is most certainly going to happen.

While Love is the most important, the emotion of Fear is one of the most powerful. Fear is our Achilles heel. Fear can grip us and lock us into paralysis, both physically and mentally. Fear is our destruct button that can stop us in our tracks and shut us down. For this reason, Fear is the most dangerous of all the human emotions. Fear always causes bad decisions. Fear degrades all the other emotions. Fear strips us of our humanity. Where Love is the life of us, Fear is the death of us. Anyone locked in Fear is not living. Fear will be discussed at length later on as well.

I have decided to include Greed as an emotion worth mentioning, because like Fear, Greed has the capacity to destroy humanity. Greed will also be discussed more at length later on. But Greed is the disease or virus implanted into the human. It is the "bug" that needs to be removed if they come out with Humans 2.0, because Greed has proven to be something all humans feel, and if acted upon, always hurts humanity.

That is quite a collection of Emotions. I could write an entire book on just Emotions. However, my goal is just to make my point in the power, intensity, and importance of Emotions to the human experience.

Between Sensations and Emotions, we can clearly see why being human is an amazing experience that any Soul would want to have, and perhaps even needs to have. Being human provides a wide expanse of experiences that totally symbolize the essence of life.

Even so, I would be remiss if I did not include the capacity of Memory, or memories, in this chapter. Memories play an important role in the Human Experience. Humans spend lots of time thinking of their memories. These memories can then initiate all of the emotions we listed. Memories is that bank of buttons at our finger tips for experiencing any array of emotions we wish to experience, without leaving the comfort of our home, chair, or bed. Just by the thought of memories, we can fully live out an experience and emotions, without even moving. How cool is that?

What is the best part of being human? Well, each person is encouraged to have their own answer, and likely does have their own answer. But for me, I think the best part of being human is the wide diverse set of Sensations and Emotions that are experienced. The

Human Experience guarantees a wild ride that will not be forgotten.

Conversely, what is the worst part of being human? Same answer. The worst part of being human is the wide array of intense emotions that can at times be very painful, uncomfortable, and draining. Being human is exhausting, difficult, and even scary at times.

But the bottom line is that being human offers a powerful experience for our Soul Energy, which allows for growth and evolution.

CHAPTER 17

Human Vulnerabilities

I will start this chapter by first commenting on the basic strength and vulnerabilities of the Universe and God. The main vulnerability of the Universe/God is that the concept and its details cannot be proven. The strength of the Universe/God is that the concept and details cannot be disproven. Science has its limitations where the Universe is concerned. Therefore, there is still lots of wiggle room for personal opinion and perception. It's much more fun that way.

Humans are not so lucky. Science has done a great job at defining and explaining humans in most every detail. This includes human psychology of course. Therefore, without as much wiggle room to wiggle, humans have to acknowledge and accept a laundry list of weaknesses and vulnerabilities. I spoke in the last chapter of the wonderful reasons to be human. Now it is time to look at the darker side. By looking closely in the mirror without pretty filters, we can more quickly learn, grow, and evolve into a better species, hopefully.

The first and most obvious vulnerability is the fact humans are organic creatures and very open to disease. Humans have open mouths and noses and congregate very closely with other humans. Humans also have hands and fingers which they use to touch everything around them, and then have a natural habit of touching their mouths and noses afterward. This set of circumstances is like a lemming marching off a cliff. It is a guarantee of illness and disease.

However, the irony is that the most serious and deadly diseases humans fall victim to, are often caused by humans themselves. Bad sanitation, self-destructive behaviors such as drinking and drug use, along with poisoning their own food with chemicals that increase the profit of sales, all contribute to humans basically poisoning themselves on purpose.

More damaging than "accidentally" poisoning and harming themselves, humans poison and harm themselves on purpose in the form of vices, or bad habits, and addictions.

Humans will literally and purposely smoke cigarettes, knowing almost for a fact that they will end up with a debilitating lung disease, or deadly cancer. Yet, humans march onward toward the cliff anyway.

Of course, we cannot delay in mentioning Drinking. Alcohol drinking obviously, which gradually kills a human over time by directly ingesting a poison.

Then there is drug use. This includes both legal and illegal drug use. Illicit drugs such as Crack and Heroine will kill anyone quicker than anything else. But Cocaine and huffing fumes are not far behind. Pills and medications used irresponsibly is the equivalent of directly poisoning yourself as well.

Humans are very vulnerable to these vices. Why is this? Well, it comes down to something that make being human a most wonderful experience. Emotions. In the earlier chapter I made the case that the range and intensity of human emotions are what makes being human worth the experience and effort.

However, these same emotions make humans very vulnerable. Humans are unable to control their emotions. The emotions are very strong, intense, and they often come and go, ebb and flow, without warning or control. Emotions are usually out of control, and sometimes in an exaggerated way.

Emotions such as anger and sadness can cause Depression and self-destructive behaviors that can be very harmful. This self-sabotaging behavior can manifest in the form of increased intensity of vices, or outright self-harm such as cutting, self-injury, or suicide.

Human emotions can become so intense and overwhelming that they literally cause a human to kill themselves. I do not know about you, but I would call that a design flaw! It is the equivalent of an electric overload that causes an automatic self-destruct sequence. Not good.

Human emotions also leave humans more vulnerable to manipulation by others. Dubious actors use a person's emotions to manipulate them into giving or doing things that a clear-thinking person would not do. Being open to manipulation is one of the biggest vulnerabilities of all and is worthy of a book of its own.

As if disease and out of control emotions are not bad enough, humans have some very insidious psychological behaviors that make them particularly vulnerable. There are many we could come up with, I am sure; but I am just going to mention a few that I think are absolutely key.

The first is Greed. Humans are never satisfied. They always want more. And more. And more. This insatiable appetite that is never satisfied is a terrible psychological behavior that results in many problems. Obviously, there is a logical reason for limits on most activities and things. Too much candy makes us sick. Cutting down too many trees destroys the Earth. Killing too many animals destroys not only the eco system, but future food sources as well. Raising prices too much can result in nobody buying your product. Cutting expenses too much result in poor quality. This concept of Greed causes humans to intentionally exceed logical smart limits. Thus, humans will intentionally engage in destructive behaviors and acts that directly hurt themselves. It is very illogical. But to be illogical is to be human.

Another one is "Group Think." Group Think is a well-researched behavior where humans tend not to think independently. I hate to use the analogy, but humans can be a little like sheep. When one sheep goes, the rest follow. Plenty of studies have been done on this. Humans are very open to the power of suggestion. If one person states an opinion that seems plausible, and a second person validates it by supporting it, the chances are good that everyone else in the group will agree and go along with it, even if they do not understand it, or fully agree on a full intellectual level.

The path of least resistance for a human is to always agree with the group. Humans seem to have a switch in their brain that shuts off all independent intellectual thought once a certain threshold of group consensus has been reached. Humans avoid confronting a group opinion. It is much easier to simply go along with the group opinion, even if the individual has not fully processed and validated it individually.

Similar to Group Think is "Tribalism." Tribalism is when a human not only goes along with the Group Think, but also aggressively agrees and supports the group's position, even if it is factually or morally wrong. What a human wants more than being right, is to be included. If you give a human a choice between being correct and alone, or wrong and liked, they will almost always go with being wrong as long as they feel included and accepted by a group.

Tribalism is why and how humans are able to justify doing horrific acts within a group, even though intellectually they may know it's wrong. Tribalism is dangerous to not only individual humans, but also humanity as a whole. Human history is littered with examples of how Group Think and Tribalism allowed great atrocities and destruction to occur without any hesitation, even though intellectually and spiritually, these same humans knew it was wrong on some deeper level. Being accepted and included in a group was more important to them than being morally or factually correct.

But I would argue there is another human vulnerability that is even more dangerous and proven to be deadlier over time. This is the psychological trait of humans needing an idol to worship. On an innocent level, humans have a need to believe in something or someone greater than themselves. This in itself seems harmless and fine. Most of us humans have some kind of religious or spiritual belief, or faith, that we hold dearly because it helps us get through hard times.

This only proves my point. The point being, that humans must have something greater, often an idol, to look up to and lead them, or guide them. This "idol" is most often a religious figure. But it can also be a business leader, gang leader, family member, or the almighty currency of money. There is always something a human chooses as being worthy of following and pursuing, even if it goes beyond logic, fact, and common sense. It can also go beyond what is moral and right.

A human without that idol seems lost and lonely without purpose. Why is this? Why must humans have some person or thing to worship or follow?

I think if you look at the psychology of it all, the answer is that humans, in concept, are unable to lead themselves. Humans seem unable to function well without an outside leader or influence. Humans also require an external force of inspiration. Humans need something or someone to look up to, or they feel lost and even despondent. Humans need to know there is someone greater than them, that know better than them, how to live. Humans need to be told what to do, and even how to think, or again, they feel lost and confused. I suppose it would be like separating a flock of sheep until each sheep is alone. How would each sheep know when to move, feed, or leave? They are used to just going with the flock without any individual thought. So alone, they might become confused and apathetic. I would say it is definitely a vulnerability when humans have not yet surpassed the psychology of a sheep.

But let us be fair. Why is this a problem? What is the harm in humans needing a higher influence or idol to worship or follow? The answer is that a group of humans blindly following an idol or leader without individual intellectual thought can be very dangerous. An idol, leader, or general group belief can be very harmful to humanity as a whole. What if the belief, idol, or leader, instructs the group to harm other humans? That is a rhetorical question obviously, since our history is full of this behavior. Religious bigotry against others, and wars, are all started based upon this behavior of following the leader, idol, or belief.

Most individual people have no desire to harm another person. But if the idol or leader instructs them to do so, the human will often do so without hesitation or independent thought. This need for an idol or leader opens humans up to brainwashing, manipulation, and being used to harm humanity.

I believe this need to mindlessly follow an idol or leader, without any individual intellectual thought or fact basis, is the great cancer of humanity. It is basically humanity killing itself from within. That brings us full circle back to the beginning where I spoke of humans purposely poisoning and harming themselves.

In short, humanity, or a human's greatest vulnerability, is their propensity to harm and kill themselves. Very ironic for one's greatest threat to be themselves.

CHAPTER 18

What Is Your Idol?

I n the previous chapter, I alluded to the fact that a major human vulnerability is the need to have some sort of Idol to look up to and follow. We need to take a closer look at that and examine the upsides as well as the downsides. At this point in human evolution, people need some sort of idol. They need something greater than themselves to look up to, guide them, and steer toward. As I have said before, humans are much like sheep in that they have a natural tendency to follow something. Most humans are afraid of being alone, so following something they view as greater than themselves, gives them comfort, and doing this with a group of other people gives them even greater comfort.

In my view, there are basically five different idols used or followed by the huge majority of humans. They are Religion, God, Specific Mentors, Nature, and Themselves. Obviously, the fifth I mentioned, "Themselves", is not following anything else so it's a violation of the entire "idol" concept, but I include it because it is what evolution is driving us to eventually. I will explain each of the four idols in detail.

RELIGION

Religion is the most common idol. This book is not about religion, nor does it aim to be pro-religion or anti-religion. Therefore, I will not be going into too much detail regarding the different religions, or my opinions of them.

With that said, a majority of humans on Earth believe in some sort of religion. There are plenty of people who do not believe in any religion, or follow any religion, but they are in the minority.

Religions are based upon a rulebook. Different religions have different rulebooks. But the general principle is that a "culture of rules" are contained in the book and they must be followed. The rulebooks illustrate the rules in the form of stories of what happens when you do not follow the rules.

Religions are based on fear and reward. Based upon the rulebook, the religion will scare its followers into following the rules by explaining or showing the awful things that will happen to them if they do not follow the rules. Whether it be not going to heaven, or going to hell, or violent punishment, the fear is ever present for those who do not follow the rules of the book.

At the same time, the rulebook promises wonderful rewards for those who follow the rules. Whether it is entry into a wonderful bountiful heaven, a guaranteed afterlife, forgiveness of all sins, validation as a person, or a multitude of virgins waiting for each man upon death, the rulebook promises wonderful things if you follow all the rules.

But of course, humans are far from perfect. Nobody can follow all the rules. So, religions have in place ways you can repent and not be punished for breaking the rules. Certain acts, deeds, punishments, or even payments to the religious organizations, can "fix" your sin or mistake, and all is well again.

I apologize if any of that sounds cynical or disrespectful. My aim is to look at this from a purely objective point of view.

However, on the cynical darker side, some religions may use their influence for dubious gain. Some religions use their influence to cause their followers to commit horrible atrocities in the name of their religion. Additionally, religions tend to use their influence to encourage or force monetary payments from their followers for the purpose of profit.

Using a "carrot and stick" approach, allows religions to have huge emotional influence over their followers. Dangling fear over their heads, while also offering amazing rewards can get most humans to do most anything.

But I will stop being cynical for a moment and look at the brighter more positive side of religion. Religions also create a very strong sense of community amongst its followers. A person can have a true sense of belonging within a religion. Many people who have no family and are quite lonely, feel a real sense of family and community by being active within their religion.

Additionally, many religions participate in charitable activities. Religions naturally raise money constantly from followers, so they have the funds to donate to good causes.

I view the advantages of having Religion as your idol to be, the fact it creates a very strong sense of community that can even replace a family. There can also be a strong sense of charity helping those less fortunate.

I view the disadvantages of having Religion as your idol to be, the fact it is based on Fear, and the fact the rulebook can contain scripture that is bigoted, discriminatory, harmful, or even violent to certain people. The fact it is based on fear also opens up the potential for manipulation and profiting from its followers.

Religion has been around forever. It is based on a faith that you believe in something that cannot be proven. It is based on rulebooks written by anonymous authors for the most part. The rulebooks are often changed over the centuries.

Most followers of religion these days tend to follow their religion to a certain degree, but not literally. Many people will tell you that they only participate in religion for the sense of community and family it offers. But there are always some that follow it because they truly believe in the rulebook and attempt to follow the rulebook to the letter of the law as much as possible.

Regardless of which religion you may follow, or your purpose for following it, it would be considered your idol if you participate in religion. Let us move onto the next idol.

GOD & THE UNIVERSE

As you will remember, we are using the terms "God" and "Universe" interchangeably, because to me they are the same thing. For the purposes of this section I will use the term "God" only but bear in mind I am also referring to the Universe as well.

Living with God as your idol is very different from living with Religion as your idol. While Religion is based upon fear and a "carrot/stick" approach, living with God as your idol is based entirely and solely on Love. Love is the language of God and the Universe. So, anything based on God, will also be based on Love.

Therefore the "rules" of living by God are very different, and yet quite simple. Using God as your idol means you live by Love. You aim to love all people and all creatures. There are no rules and no exceptions to this. There is no discrimination, and you operate under the concept of inclusion rather than exclusion.

When you do not know what to do, you simply ask, "What would God do?" You will also hear some people following this type of spirituality saying, "What would Jesus do?" It is a sticky wicket bringing Jesus into this because that references religion. But some who believe in following God, also believe Jesus was a real historical figure.

Jesus has obviously been adopted by the Christian religion as their idol. But outside of that, Jesus is seen as a real historical figure who we can look at independently from any religion. Additionally, since God has never been viewed as an actual earthly person, looking to Jesus as God's face allows us to better relate to God. So, whether you want to only consider God, or whether you want to consider Jesus as the face of God, both are relevant to the type of spirituality I am discussing. Also, as I discuss all this, keep in mind that Muhammad would be inserted as the direct prophet of God, rather than Jesus, if you follow Islam. But for simplicity sake, I am going to continue with the Christian - Jesus example.

Either way, God and Jesus by most all accounts can be viewed as Loving entities that aimed to teach, love, and support those who follow them. God as the Universe is exactly that. It is a collection of soul energy that yearns to learn, grow, and evolve, while engaging in the language of love, for which is the language of the Universe.

Living with God as our idol forces us to set aside any bigotry, discrimination, or hate toward others. It forces us to do what God and Jesus would have done, which is to listen, comprehend, guide, support, accept, forgive, and love, without exception.

If we make mistakes and fall short of this nearly impossible goal, we simply learn, grow, and try harder in the future. There are no pennants, payments, or punishments necessary. No fear scare tactics are involved, but also no amazing rewards offered. It is simply a Universal law and handshake.

People who are deeply into a religion often cannot understand how a person outside of religion can still feel so close to God. Hopefully this is explaining that concept, because indeed people with this spirituality are very close to God, always asking and thinking what God would do, and trying to stay in alignment with those values.

I view the advantages of living with God as your idol to be, the fact it is based solely on love rather than fear, as well as inclusion rather than exclusion, and does not include any bigotry or discrimination. The other advantage is that you are not tethered to a rulebook that you are constantly in danger of violating.

I view the disadvantage of living with God as your idol to be, the fact it is a solitary experience. It is up to the individual to create the bond with God and follow it without the prompting of a "leader." The biggest disadvantage in my view is that it does not offer the sense of community and family that Religion offers.

Now onto our next idol.

MENTORS

Some people do not see Religion or God/Universe as viable idols. They might not believe in religion or God and are not engaged with the concept of the Universe. But that does not leave them immune from the common human need for an idol.

Thus, they often choose and adopt a person important to them to be their idol. In a very cute way, we often see examples of this in young children who look up to their older sibling. They may be too young to fully understand and engage with religion and God, but they totally understand the concept of the Mentor, which in their case could be an older sibling.

A Mentor can be a variety of people. It might be a sibling, parent, teacher, friend, sports hero, music or entertainment hero, human legend, or an actual mentor in the business or educational sense. But the point is that this person ends up being the one person they look up to most.

The follower tends to mimic the behavior of the idol. This can be a double-edged sword depending on the actual behavior of the idol.

The advantage of having a Mentor as your idol is that your idol is an actual person that you may be able to have personal contact with. This creates a very close bond with your idol and access which is impossible with the previously mentioned idols.

The obvious disadvantage of a Mentor as an idol, is that nobody is perfect, and the follower will start to mimic any bad behavior which the idol exhibits. We see this with gang leaders being an idol for young kids, and then the young kids want to be in a gang. We see this with sports heroes who end up disappointing us with their behavior.

When having a Mentor as an idol, one must be careful to choose carefully and have the ability to change their idol should something go wrong with their current idol. It is a slippery slope for sure, but a common idol for many people, especially those who do not believe in Religion, God, or understand the Universe.

Our next idol is what I call, the Ancient Idol.

NATURE

Having Nature, or the Earth, as your idol is from the ancient ways. Honestly, I think it is also the most genuine balanced idol of them all so far. Having Nature or the Earth as your idol means you are putting yourself in total alignment with Nature. You are in tune with all that is around you, including the animals, the Earth, and the weather.

Being in tune with Nature and following the cues of Nature is a very peaceful and Zen experience. As an American, I point to the Native Americans as being the masters at using Nature as an idol. The Native Americans took clues and cues from all the animals, birds, sky, and everything around them. They respected Nature, hoping it would respect them back in the form of providing what they needed to survive. They lived one with Nature.

Living with Nature as your idol is about a mutual respect for Nature, being in tune with Nature, and seeking all your signs from Nature. In my opinion, it is probably most closely in alignment with how humans were intended to behave and exist.

I call Nature the ancient idol, because it no longer exists on a grand scale. In fact, the opposite exists. Humans now exploit Nature for profit, even if it means absolute destruction of Nature. Humans have abandoned being in alignment with Nature, and instead invest in technologies to destroy Nature for the most convenient short-term gains. It is an interesting turn evolution has taken indeed.

But still the same, I keep Nature in this book as a major idol because it once was a major idol, it should still be a major idol, and there are still some very spiritual people who use Nature as their idol.

Now for our final idol, and most difficult.

SELF

Living with "Self" as your idol is perhaps a paradox. How can your idol be yourself? This concept is difficult for many humans. However, it is important I discuss it because it is likely the future for humans as we continue to evolve.

Living with your own sense of self as your moral compass means you must self-define all your precepts. You must create your own guiding principles. You must create your own moral values, your own rules. You must have totally developed your own sense of self and fully understand yourself, your goals, your values, your weaknesses, and your own inspirations. Basically, you must be the master of your own self. You must be able to think independently and have the self-discipline to enforce your own values upon yourself.

Living with Self as your idol means having no external force to look up to, and nobody to tell you what to do, or how to behave. It means self-correcting when you go wrong. Imagine having the discipline to do this effectively. Living with Self-means being a self-contained unit who knows what they believe in, why they believe in it, where they are going, and why they are going there. It means knowing the guidelines, rules, and values you have decided to follow, and to provide your own self-discipline to abide by them.

Perhaps this is beginning to sound like utopia or impossible. I agree it sounds difficult, but it is certainly not impossible. Some among us already engage in this to some degree. It is always a work in progress. I could probably write an entire book on just this perhaps.

The advantages of living with Self as yourself idol are tremendous. You are free from all external manipulation, control, and interference. You maintain strong independent thought at all times. You get to define your own set of values that you want to live by. You have amazing freedom in living how you want to live. You are truly the master of your own self.

The disadvantages are also obvious. It is extremely difficult to do this. It requires a person to have great independence of thought, creativity, confidence, self-awareness, and amazing discipline. You pretty much need to be a Jedi.

But a Jedi is very cool, yes? Imagine if everyone had the strength of character to live this way. There would be no more "sheep mentality" or groups ganging up on other groups. Each individual would be guided by independent thought rather than dangerous "group think."

In other words, we would have more highly evolved humans living in a more highly evolved society. But much work and evolution would need to happen first for the majority of the populace to choose this type of idol.

So, there are your five idol concepts. Perhaps you will consider which is your idol, and maybe you even have a mixture of more than one. That is entirely possible as well. But if you have none of the above, you are likely not human.

CHAPTER 19

Good Vs. Evil

Wikipedia defines "Good" as: In its most general context, the concept of good denotes that conduct which is to be or should be preferred when posed with a choice between a set of possible actions. Good is generally considered to be the opposite of evil.

Wikipedia defines "Evil" as: Evil, in a general sense, is the opposite or absence of good. It can be an extremely broad concept, though in everyday usage is often used more narrowly to denote profound wickedness.

In my opinion, those definitions are kind of wordy. I wanted to make it easier for people to understand the different between Good and Evil. Right and Wrong. So here it is.

Good is Love. Evil is Fear.

When something is coming out of a place of love, or done out of love, or love is intended, then it is Good. When something is coming out of a place of fear, or done to make people fear, or creating fear, then it is Evil. Is that simple enough? Love vs. Fear.

Feel free to take my definition for a test drive to see how it feels. Run down different scenarios in your mind, determine if you are feeling love, or feeling fear, then label it Good or Evil. See if it works.

This world is a tricky place. It is full of dubious people who are always trying to accomplish something by labeling things as Good, when they are not necessarily good. Conversely, there are many people who are often persecuted and slandered as bad, but they are actually good.

Good people come in many colors, shapes, and sizes. Dirty, full of tattoos, scary clothes and hair, nicely dressed in suits, dressed in clergy uniforms, politicians, and the list goes on.

Evil people also come in many colors, shapes, and sizes. Dirty, full of tattoos, scary clothes and hair, nicely dressed in suits, dressed in clergy uniforms, politicians, and the list goes on.

Oh wait. Those lists above for good people and bad people are the same. Yes, they are. So how can I tell who is good and who is bad? Which clergy is good and which clergy is bad? Which tattoo covered scary looking dude is good and which is bad? Well, how do they act toward you? Do they come from a place of love, extend love, and make you feel love? Or do they come from a place of fear, extend fear, and make you feel fear? That is how to tell.

We will take clergy for an example because I feel it is the best example. If someone of the clergy talked to me about how I should fear God and I will go to hell if I do not shape up and do what he says, I would say that is coming from a place of fear. However, if a clergy told me to feel the love of God, and know God loves me no matter what, then I would feel that is coming from a place of love. I would then know which clergy is good and which is not. This example applies to everyone.

Let us now look at some symbols of good and evil. Satan is viewed as a symbol of evil. What does Satan look like? Is Satan a red monster with horns? Or is Satan a figurative symbol of evil things and evil people? Or is Satan a person on earth who does evil things? I always find it interesting how people refer to Satan and the Anti-Christ as the same thing. Yet, Satan is a red monster with horns, and the Anti-Christ is a yet to be known clever businessman in a suit who will make us think he is our savior before he destroys us. The monster with horns sounds more mythological, while the clever evil man in the suit sounds like some people I've seen here on Earth in my everyday life. But we know both are evil because they come from a place of fear with fearful evil intentions.

Now for some symbols of good. Many view Jesus Christ as a symbol of good, regardless of your religious nature. By many accounts, Jesus was a modest man of modest means, wearing a simple gown, and getting by as a carpenter. But Jesus was preaching love and came from a place of love. Therefore, Jesus is a symbol of good. Mother Teresa is another symbol of good. She was a living angel who only gave from love. A simple older woman living a simple life. Yet, she was drenched in so much love, making her deserving of Sainthood.

When people point to things and tell me they are good and bad, I do not just accept that judgment. If you point to a homeless person and say they are bad, I would ask, "What does the homeless person do and how do they treat other people?" If a homeless person gives his only coat to another homeless person because they needed it more, then I would say the homeless person is a symbol of good because they acted out of love. If someone points to a place of worship and says it is good, but I come to find out it preaches hate against other people, then I would say it is a symbol of evil. When I see a nice-looking person in a suit, I will not know if they are good or evil until I witness their actions and intentions.

Nobody should be judged without given a chance to show their intentions and actions of either love or fear. Then once they show which card they are playing, you can know what you are dealing with. This applies to the lowest most disadvantaged of our society, as well as the wealthiest most powerful of our society. They each have an equal chance at being good or evil, depending on whether they act out of a place of love or a place of fear. The Universe is a light and dark place. It is full of good and evil. Good and evil is everywhere, including within ourselves. Examine your inner thoughts and memories. There are times you have used fear against someone to get what you wanted. There are times you have used love unconditionally because you knew it was the right thing. In this example, you have acted with evil intent, and acted with good intent. We are human, and we are all over the place with our emotions and behavior.

The purpose of this chapter is not to cure and banish evil from the Universe. That is not likely to happen. My purpose here is to make it easier and more obvious for you to recognize good and evil when you see it.

Instead of the "smell test," we have the "feel test." Ask yourself how something makes you feel. Do you feel love, or do you feel fear? That is the easiest way to tell if something is good or evil.

When you detect evil, you can step back and block it so that you do not fall victim to it. When you detect good, you can trust that it's okay to step closer and check things out further. This can be used in business, relationships, choosing a spiritual outlet, buying a car, almost anything.

You want to get to the point where you are in alignment with only good things. When you get good at detecting good vs. evil, you will naturally by reflex, either move away quickly, or step closer. There are no guarantees, and we are all fooled from time to time, but this is a better guide than trying to look at how someone appears and taking a wild hopeful guess of their intentions.

Most importantly of all, we all must police ourselves and constantly monitor as to whether we are acting from a place of love or a place of fear. Look at how you treat others and how you treat yourself. Always strive to be coming from a place of love so that you can be a symbol of good for the Universe and humanity.

CHAPTER 20

Your Place In The Universe

Have you wondered what your place in the Universe might be? Why are you here? What is your purpose? What are you doing here?

Humans often feel lost and wander aimlessly. Sometimes it is helpful to take a step back and see if we can make some sense of it all. We will try to do that now. Why are you here? Humans are host bodies for your soul. Your soul's goal is to have as many varied experiences as possible so that it may learn, grow, and evolve. So really, the point of your existence is driven by your Soul, not your body, or your opinionated brain. A soul does not necessarily care what specific experiences it has, as long as it has them. So, this is where you and your opinionated brain get to have some influence.

But really, it is not about our opinionated brain. It is more about what our emotions are dictating. Humans are led by their emotions. While your soul is gaining experience, your human life is allowing you to experience all the emotions and amazing things that humans get to feel and experience. Why not enjoy the ride?

So here is my take. I believe we are here to enjoy the human adventure while our souls are gaining as much experience as possible so that our souls can learn, grow, and evolve. So, it is a dual purpose. Our soul is all business and needs to experience things to evolve. But we also get to feel and experience the journey of being human in such a diverse species, environment, and world. Business and pleasure. Like a mullet, business in front and party in the back. So, make the most out of both.

So that is why you are here in principle. But as I said, your soul does not care as much what experiences it is having, so long as it is having them. That means you, your mind, emotions, and preferences, get to decide which experiences you have.

Ideally, a person would go through a deep well considered process to determine which adventures they want to have. At this point, we set aside our soul. Our soul is fine and just wants adventure. We need to now fully consider our human existence to figure out the rest. So, let us do that.

The first step is to know thyself. What excites you? What inspires you? What interests you? Answer those three questions. Then you need to take inventory of yourself. You need to determine your strengths, weakness, available resources, and such things. But wait, this is starting to feel like a Hunter Equation moment. So here we go.

After answering the three questions I asked above, you should start coming up with some ideas for your desired Future Outcomes. Again, base your Future Outcomes on what excites you, what inspires you, and what interests you. Think hard. There are no wrong answers. No limitations yet.

Now look at your Intent. What would like to do? What fills you with love? Remember, Intent is about love and positivity. So, what in life fills you with love and positivity? List some of those things under Intent. Then, look at Actions. What Actions would be most fun for you to do? What Actions would you enjoy taking? What Actions are realistic and possible for you to do? What Actions are impossible for you to do? You are looking for the Actions you would enjoy taking, while having them realistic and possible to do, based upon the inventory of yourself that you took.

Next, you are looking at the External Forces involved. These are both good and bad. Good External Forces might be family connections or opportunities you have. What advantages do you have, simply due to your circumstances in life? Conversely, what things out there would be blocking you and making certain things difficult or impossible? Look at all that stuff and cross-reference them with each other. Hopefully, you can find some positive External Forces that might help your possible Actions, and spot some very negative External Forces that might rule out some of your possible Actions.

Finally, we have the Random Luck factor that reminds us that life often leads us to places we never expected. Keep this in mind and be open to the fact you do not have total control over your life. Things will happen you do not expect. So, expect that.

Your scratch paper should be full of notes and cross outs and questions marks. Hopefully, you have some key words and ideas that have not been crossed out. Clean up your equation and see what you are left with. That should give you an idea of some directions and passions you might want to consider in life. This process might very well give you your purpose in life; or tell you what you should be doing here while you are here.

So let us see, so far we have your soul which is here for business gaining any experiences it can, your human life is here to enjoy the ride of being human, and you have taken inventory and given thought about your "Self" to figure out what you should be doing here while you are alive.

Now you can look at how you want to live. Consider laying out some guidelines and rules for yourself. Who or what will be your idol, if anyone or anything? We took an entire chapter to discuss this.

What type of values and morals do you want to live by? This is not a rhetorical question. This is a real genuine question. For example, a person who wants to be the greatest richest businessman in the world, will likely have values that state, "I can do anything necessary for success as long as nobody dies in the process." Some would not even worry about if someone dies in the process. Conversely, someone who feels a passion for serving people might say, "I won't do anything that hurts another person." These are two very different value structures. Both are valid, and both are commonly used. There is plenty of room in between those as well. So, what is your value and moral structure? Give it lots of thought and decide what kind of person you want to be, and make sure it is in alignment with your life purpose you worked out with the Hunter Equation.

Next, you want to consider that your soul is not the only thing that wants to learn and grow. Most humans on an emotional level also want to learn and grow. Give some thought on your feelings about education, spiritual growth, ascension, evolution, and things like that. Decide which of those, if any, you have a passion in pursuing. Obviously, it is easier to start on a path of intense education when we are younger, but that is not always the case, and life does not always work out that way. But my point is that the sooner you figure out what you want to engage in, the better.

Finally, think about what lasting changes you would like to make in this world. How would you like to leave your mark on this world in this human life? Will you be able to affect change in a direction you wish to see it go? What contribution can you make to humanity while you are here? Consider ways you can leave a lasting mark on this world so that your stamp is here long after you are gone.

Do not be afraid to be unique, take risks, and express yourself. When I asked, what your place in the universe is, I mean for you to answer that yourself. But part of the answer is that you must make your own place in the Universe. So, make it.

What is the meaning of life? The ideal meaning of life is to make a positive difference while enjoying the journey.

CHAPTER 21

Using The Hunter Equation In Your Life

Peeople approach life in different ways. Some people just live life as it comes and learn things the hard way from mistakes. Other people carefully calculate everything before each move and hope their calculations are correct. Others figure that as long as they think positive thoughts, they can do anything they want, and positive things will come into their life.

All of the above approaches use a piece of the Hunter Equation. Just to remind, the Hunter Equation is:

Future Outcome =
(Intent + Actions + External Forces + Random Luck)

People who just kind of glide through life, and suffer the consequences as they go, tend to react to External Forces, while they are at the mercy of Random Luck. People who carefully calculate their every move, tend to focus mostly on what Actions they will be taking, not realizing that their logical outcome will never happen because the External Forces and Random Luck of the Universe will make sure they do not happen. Those who think the positive thinking of Law of Attraction is all you need, are mostly just focusing on Intent, while they have disappointments waiting for them as Random Luck ravages their happy day.

There are many possible life strategies and approaches, but most all of them only give heavy weight to one or two of the Hunter Equation components. This is why most people in life struggle and experience disappointment, despite their best well intended efforts. Life does not work on one or two elements. It is just not that simple, and it is just not that easy.

Life operates on all four elements of the Hunter Equation. For this reason, it is only logical that we carefully take into account all four elements with our approach to life. Yes, it makes life more complicated. But it makes life better and gives us a better possible outcome.

Using the Hunter Equation requires a shift in thinking. Most people are used to thinking in one or two dimensions. What I mean by this is they are used to thinking about keeping their intent (attitude) positive, or just thinking about what actions they are taking; or just reacting to all the external forces being thrown at them. With the Hunter Equation, you have to shift your thinking to multi-dimensional. You need to be able to imagine all four balls in the air at the same time. You need to be able to consider all four elements at the same time and view how they may react to each other. This is not easy and may take practice.

My suggestion on proceeding is to first be sure you have all four elements memorized so they are automatic. Then, whenever you encounter a life decision or life problem, you train yourself to first take a breath, take a pause, and this shall be your cue to recall the four elements of the Hunter Equation. Then consider each of the elements in how to proceed with a life challenge, or how to solve a life problem.

I will now talk about different ways the Hunter Equation can be used for different life situations. This will hopefully give you a better idea of how to apply the Hunter Equation, and some practical scenarios of how it would be done.

MANIFESTING & ACHIEVING A GOAL OR DESIRED RESULT

Historically, we have all been taught that if you want to manifest, achieve goals, or set a goal, what you need to do is write them down, think positive thoughts, and take regular action toward those goals. It's not such a horrible approach really.

However, under the Hunter Equation, let us look at it this way. Firstly, clearly define what you want your Future Outcome to be. What are you manifesting? What do you want to achieve? What is your desired end result? Remember, the equation actually starts with "Future Outcome =" So clearly define what you want your Future Outcome to be.

Secondly, set your Intent. In setting your Intent, look at what your intent is for this goal. Why do you want this Future Outcome? What do you think this goal or outcome will give you, or do for you? What is your expectation? All of these questions are part of your analytical portion of your Intent. Then set your attitude intent. This requires applying Love to the Intent, the goal, the Future Outcome. Love this Future Outcome and embrace it. Feel the positivity around it. Feel the positive feelings you will have after you achieve your goal.

Next, you want to examine the Actions required. First, examine the analytical side of the Actions required. This means do your research. Know what is required in achieving the goal you set. Research, read, ask questions, and learn. Know the actual Actions. Then, you want to look at the Actions and apply Love to them. This is done in order to inspire you to take these Actions. Become inspired and excited about taking all the required Actions.

Notice above how we looked at Intent and Actions separately, but then we looked at them in a combined way as well.

Now we have our Intent set and we are feeling the love; and we have our Actions mapped out, and we are feeling inspired to do them.

Now we look at External Forces. Looking at External Forces means playing Devil's Advocate. Consider, and even write down, all possible External Forces that could possibly affect your plan. Basically, what are all the things that could go wrong? This of course would be a violation of the Law of Attraction to do this. It is why I love this part of the process so much, and why you have now stepped beyond the Law of Attraction into a much more effective process. Now you are taking into account all the possible downsides, limitations, and things that could upset the apple cart. You are anticipating the potential problems and limitations.

After you have taken into account all the possible External Forces you can think of, you want to work backwards. Meaning, you now want to look at what potential Actions could be taken in response to such External Forces. This would be called Contingency Planning by most. So, get your Contingency Plans (Actions) in place. Then walk back another step and revisit Intent by showing all your Contingency Plans some Love and positive thought, by knowing you have done the work to anticipate problems, and that you should feel good about yourself for doing this.

Finally, consider Random Luck. This is a reminder that even the best-laid plans may not work. There are no guarantees in life. When thinking of Random Luck, you want to first consider that External Forces can change the equation at any time Randomly, by luck or bad luck. Most importantly, you want to assess if there are any Actions you can take to increase your odds of success. In other words, can you take any Actions that might put luck a little more in your favor? Luck is about probability. So, any Actions you can take to move luck more into your favor is a good thing. Then step back again into Intent and show that Random Luck some Love. Always love that dice before you throw it.

At this point, you have a complete Goal Setting task done by using the Hunter Equation. Good job. You can see how you would have taken into account many different things. You remembered to look at all four elements sitting in the air, all at the same time. You also interacted all the elements with each other, going forwards and backwards, and forwards again.

Now remember this. The Hunter Equation is a Universal equation from the Universe. This means it is alive and always moving. Certainly, Random Luck and External Forces are always changing, because those are two things you do not control. So always keep an eye on your equation, as it changes and shifts. When you see changes in your equation, revisit all the elements to make any necessary changes. When one element changes, it affects the other elements, along with your Future Outcome. So always keep an eye on that equation and be ready to make changes as needed. That is real life. I again apologize for life being so complicated and difficult. I'm truly sorry. I too, wish that I could just think positive thoughts, go to work every day, and have my life turn out like roses. It would be wonderful. Too bad, too sad, it does not work that way. But hopefully now you have a more advanced accurate template to work with for better Future Outcomes.

CAREER/JOB

Let us look at applying the Hunter Equation to maximizing career, job growth, and benefits.

If you want to do well in your career, you can use the Hunter Equation to improve your Future Outcome. Obviously, your Future Outcome will be to thrive in your career or job, meaning promotion and pay most likely. But please be as specific as possible in defining the Future Outcome you are seeking.

Then look at your Intent. First the analytical side. Revisit why you want this Future Outcome relating to your job. Are you sure you really want it? Are you sure you even want this job? If you hate your career or job, then this exercise is pointless, and you need to go backwards and find a new career. So first confirm that you are solid in your chosen career and that you indeed want the defined Future Outcome. Now that you have confirmed that you truly believe in this career and this Future Outcome, you can show it an outpouring of Love and positive thoughts.

Next, what Actions are required to reach this Future Outcome? Any specific training? Certifications? Approval from a specific person? You know the drill. Write it all down. Consider all the possible Actions you must take to get this done. Then show those Actions some Love. Get inspired to do them. Be inspired to do them.

Now consider all the External Forces that may push back against your plan. This might mean considering certain people, bosses, co-workers that might try to block you or sabotage you. Do not just think positive thoughts, bury your head in the sand, and hope for the best. Instead, face your demons and consider all the possible blocks, problems, and difficulties.

Then take one step back and consider your Actions or your contingency plans to deal with such External Forces. For example, if you can anticipate being blocked or sabotaged by a certain person, then be one step ahead of the process, and put an Action into place now, which deals with that person, meaning that External Force. Maybe you can even prevent this person from being a problem if you have an Action in place now which deals with them before it's even a problem. Look at how smart you are being and show it all some Love. Good attitude still matters, especially to the boss. So, keep that positive Intent.

Then remind yourself of that ugly Random Luck. Realize anything can go wrong at any time. Consider the ways your luck could go against you. Then consider any Actions you can take to increase the probability of good luck in this matter. Show those dice some love before you throw them. With any luck, you just improved your chances at a better Future Outcome for your Career and job.

I went slightly faster through that process. Hopefully you are getting the hang of this.

SOLVING PROBLEMS

When solving a problem using the Hunter Equation, first clearly understand and define the problem. Your Future Outcome is going to be how you want the situation to look *after* the problem is solved. In many cases, the Future Outcome will be stated as the exact opposite of the problem. So, for example, if your problem was "I don't have a car," your Future Outcome would be stated as "I have a car." Of course, a problem is not always an object, but very often a situation. But you get the idea.

Look at your Intent. Analytically, is this truly a problem? Or is it just an unfortunate circumstance you can live with? Be sure you truly understand your problem, and that it is truly a problem. Many times, we have a bad situation and we see it as a major problem, but then days later realize it is not really a problem and it is just something bad we did not like, and we are over it and moved on from it. In your Intent, be sure you truly have a confirmed genuine problem in front of you.

Then consider the Intent with which you want to solve it. With problem solving, there are almost always multiple ways to approach the problem. Determine if your Intent is to solve the problem by replacing something, fixing something, ignoring something, or pretending it does not bother you at all. Once you decide how you want to think about it, show it some Love and own your choice.

Next, look at your Actions you think you will take to solve this problem. By this time, your problem should be well defined, you have confirmed you actually need to solve it, and you have decided what mental approach to take in solving it. So, the Actions you need to take should be narrowed down and easier to come up with than you might first suspect.

So, determine all your possible Actions, then show them some Love and realize taking these Actions might be for the best anyways, and thus be inspired and excited to take them.

But now consider all your External Forces. Who or what is going to stand in your way in solving this? Determine those obstacles. Then review your Actions or contingency plans to deal with those External Forces. Show it all some Love.

Realize life is difficult and that things do not go as planned and be aware that Random Luck might mess with you. Take the Actions that increase the probability of success. Take any Actions you can think of which anticipate problems from External Forces. Keep the Love flowing and stay positive in the knowledge that you are doing everything you can to solve your problem.

Watch your equation as it changes and shifts. When problem solving, it can shift very quickly, and often. Be sure to change with it.

RELATIONSHIPS

The Hunter Equation can be applied to your relationships. Probably the trickiest part of applying it to relationships is defining the Future Outcome you actually want. So, you will need to come up with whatever it is that you are truly after. Whether it is "I want more love in my relationship," or "I want to stop fighting," or "I want more sex," etc, you need to clearly determine it. So carefully consider your Future Outcome. Having something like "I want a happy relationship" is not totally invalid, but it is also not very specific. The more vaguely stated the Future Outcome is, the more ephemeral, and out of control your equation will be. So, keep that in mind. Tight definitions equal tighter equations. Tighter equations equal easier management, and better chances of success.

Look at your Intent. Are you sure this is what you *need*? Are you sure this is what you *want*? Are you sure this is the most important aspect of the relationship to focus on first? Are you sure this is truly important to you? Then commit to your choice. Own it. Love it. Smile. Be positive.

Now determine those Actions you need to take. This is so important in relationships. So often in relationships we bitch and moan about things, wish for them to get better, but then do nothing to actually change things ourselves. We hope the other person changes, or we even demand the other person changes. So, with the Hunter Equation, *you* need to determine the Actions *you* are going to take to achieve your stated Future Outcome. Commit to those Actions and carry them out with Love. Carrying out those Actions with resentment will not work.

Anticipate any External Forces that may affect your plans. Take them into account. Do not expect the other person to be all over you with appreciation for what you are doing. External Forces are about what may go wrong most of the time. So, consider the things you may have missed or not taken into account. Try to go back and take Actions to prevent these External Forces. Do it with Love in your heart, matching your Intent.

Life does not always serve us what we are expecting, so realize Random Luck might change the situation on you. Be prepared for this to possibly happen. Consider the External Forces that might be involved and be ready to take new Actions. Stay positive and keep the faith.

When human relationships are involved, feelings, and emotions, the equation can change instantly and often. Care is needed in monitoring this, and patience is often needed even more. But applying the Hunter Equation to your relationship is surely better than not applying it at all.

CHILDREN

For those who have children, nothing is more important than the kids (at least I hope this is the case). Therefore, applying your best thinking to your children only makes sense. So why not apply the Hunter Equation to them? You can do this in two ways. You can use the equation to improve their lives, or you can actually teach them the Hunter Equation. For right now, let's take a brief look at how we would apply the equation to your children, if you have any.

You should know the drill by now. Choose and define your Future Outcome. Whether it is to correct a behavior, a bad habit, improve grades, or what have you.

Check your Intent on this. Is this Future Outcome in alignment with what the child wants? If you are doing a Future Outcome that conflicts with the child's own desires or best interests, it probably won't work. So, check your Intent is in alignment with the child, and something truly wanted and needed by the child. Then increase your level of Love, including to the child.

Figure out all your Actions that are needed. Remember, these are Actions YOU take. This is not about dumping all kinds of unsolicited Actions upon the child. Obviously, the child may need to participate in some of the Actions, but that is all the more reason why the Future Outcome must be in alignment with the child's wishes, so that they will cooperate with you.

Look at any External Forces you face. They might be distractions, behavioral problems, or other people. Anticipate all this. Walk it backwards to try and mitigate the problems before they happen through Actions. Do all this with Love. Let the child see the Love.

Random Luck may change the situation and your plans. Be prepared for that and be patient if it happens. Be ready to adjust your equation at any time. I am hoping at this point you have the general idea of how to use the equation. You can use the equation in most any situation, problem, and circumstance.

The important thing to remember is to always keep all four elements up in front of you, and to go forwards and backwards cross referencing with each of the elements like we have done. All the elements relate to each other and support each other. When one changes, the entire equation changes. Remember the equation is a living thing, so it will bend and change. Be ready and willing to adjust. Using the Hunter Equation in your life puts you in better alignment with how the Universe works. Thus, using the equation should give you better results in your life.

CHAPTER 22

When You Get Stuck In Life

All of us get stuck in life from time to time. So, let us pretend for a moment that you have been a good person, working hard, using the Hunter Equation, and you still find yourself stuck in a bad situation or circumstances.

Now if we were one of those other theories or motivational books, we would just brush you under the rug and hope you do not come out and rain on our Law of Attraction positivity party. But fortunately, we are not doing that. We are on the real-life train, and we expect difficulty, and understand we can work through anything using the elements of the Universe. So, if you find life not working for you, whatever it is, or you find yourself stuck for some reason, here is what you should do. The first thing you should suspect is that there is something wrong with your equation. Thus, you need to have a close look at your equation. Look at each element separately in slow motion.

Is the Future Outcome you asked for realistic? Is it moral, and right? Does it somehow hurt other people? Does it hurt you?

Evaluate carefully if your Future Outcome is something you should be truly wanting and expecting. Often, people find the Future Outcome is flawed because it is harmful in some way, and the Universe is using External Forces to block it from happening. How can the Universe block you by using External Forces, you ask? Well remember, the Universe consists of living Universal Energy, including Soul Energy. This energy is connected to the Universe Energy Collective, the Akashic records, and Soul energy of everyone. If some of that energy is opposed to your Future Outcome, it can exert energy (force) upon your equation and rain on your parade. The living Universal Energy can be clever about how it throws its weight around. It can use other people to do its bidding, or other events. Never underestimate the ability of the Universe to influence things, such as your equation. Thus, one must examine their Future Outcome for possible flaws.

Then check your Intent. Is your Intent sincere and genuine, or are you just going through the motions? Your Intent must be confirmed by your soul as authentic and truly desired by you. It must be filled with love. If your Intent is void of love, or worse yet, has resentment or revenge to it, then it will not work, and that part of the equation will be broken. So, check for a genuine desire, and for love.

Then check your Actions. Have you correctly identified all the needed Actions, or did you miss one or two? Have you executed all the Actions correctly, or are there still some left undone? Were you hoping everything would work out for you without having to take all the Actions? Well that did not work, so finish the rest of the Actions. Are the Actions done with love, or are they done with resentment or disdain? Remember, all Actions must be dipped in love.

Examine the External Forces that seem to be blocking you and making you stuck. What are they? What is their origin? Can you clear them? Can you focus on the core cause, core problem, and clear the problem to clear the External Force? Can you go around, under, or over the External Force? Is the External Force trying to protect you from a flawed Future Outcome?

Review the Random Luck factor. Is bad luck the reason you are stuck? Or is it more the other elements? If it is all bad luck, then try it all again. If bad luck is not the primary culprit, then go back to the other elements above.

Basically, you need to try and fix your equation.

What if you cannot fix your equation, or life is still not working? Here is something else to try. Do what we do when your car is stuck in the mud. You rock it back, and, forth right? Give it just a little gas forward, but then let it rock backwards, then gas again forwards. You get that rocking motion going to try and get unstuck. I use what is called "Push - Pull." The Push Pull theory is something I made up myself as a joke. But it is not a joke. It seems to work. In a way, it is based on Newton's Law of "For every action, there is an equal and opposite reaction." It became an inside joke for those who know me best, because it was me going directly against the Law of Attraction. It does this because by using Push Pull, I end up thinking negative thoughts or pushing for the opposite of what I want. What this does is it rocks my car back and forth. Think about it. I first wanted a certain outcome, but it did not happen (gas pedal to go forward). But then I think of not wanting the outcome at all, and even push back against it with negative thoughts (letting the car rock backwards). Then I quietly watch for any reaction from others or the Universe that might allow me an opportunity to quickly press on the gas forward again to go forward toward the outcome I wanted.

What I have found is that very often I can manifest or attain a desired result by pushing back against it, then it sometimes will bounce back again the other way and I can use that momentum to then push it forward again. It is like a Jedi mind trick, but really it is also physics. It will also annoy your Law of Attraction friends as they watch you push against what you want, only to see you grab it again and push it forward to success as it rocks back your way. Like a pendulum in a way. This Push Pull trick takes practice. Like getting your car out of the mud, it does not always work. Sometimes you need a tow truck. But very often it does work, and you have been clever.

An example of how this works in real life is when you are dating, and it is not going well, so you play hard to get. By actually pushing *against* what you want, you can sometimes more easily bring it in. Playing hard to get can sometimes work when in a difficult dating situation under certain circumstances. Or it can get you stuck even more. You have seen it and you get the picture. But this would be Push Pull in motion as well.

The other thing to try is Time. As they often say, if you don't like the weather, just wait a bit and it will change. Same with life. Nothing stays the same. This is a double-edged sword of course. But when things are not going well, use Time to your advantage. Wait. Be like a snail hiding in its shell. Then when it is safe, you can try to crawl away. What a horrible example. Oh well. But you get what I mean hopefully.

Patience is required of course, but sometimes all we have left is just waiting it out. Give time a chance to fix things for you. Time will always change things. That is a guarantee. Very often time changes it for the worse. But when you are stuck, and things are not good, Time becomes your friend and any change is usually beneficial.

What else can you do when you are stuck? Well, ask a friend. Seek advice. Ask for help. Friends can see things from a different perspective and in their own way spot the problem which is obvious to them but was invisible to you.

Or ask an expert like me for advice. That is what we are here for. If I cannot figure out what is broken with my car, I do not just jiggle everything myself and hope time will fix it. I go see an expert who knows about cars. So, go see an expert in whatever field you are having problems with. Perhaps this should be step 1. But as a man, we will never ask for directions until we are completely lost right? So, I put this suggestion near the end.

While you are working all this out, remember to keep love in your heart. That is the language of God and the Universe after all. So maybe the Universe will speak to you and give you an answer to your problem. But you must be speaking the language of the Universe to understand what it says. The only way to do this is to be in tune with love. Be kind to yourself. Keep love in your heart. Keep the faith. Things work out or change at some point. Always.

CHAPTER 23

Humans Who Struggle Vs. Those Who Don't

Why is it that some people just seem to have one bad thing after another happen to them, while others seem to glide through life with nothing but blessings?

Great question. Wish I knew the answer! Ah, just joking. I will answer it now. I will give you my theory on it anyways. Like most answers to complex questions, there are various factors involved. Let's go through them, starting at the beginning.

You will recall a Soul's purpose in reincarnating is to gain experiences so that it can learn, grow, and evolve. Some souls have gained more experience than others have. Think of a soul as a student in school. A student just starting in school has easier classes that are less challenging. The less challenging classes still give the student new knowledge that allows them to learn and grow. Conversely, an experienced student who has already been through many classes and experiences, takes more advanced courses so that they may be adequately challenged. Some students take very advanced difficult classes that seem impossibly difficult for many of us.

The same applies with souls. Different soul energy collections have different levels and amounts of experiences. Some souls do not require as many complex experiences in order to learn and grow. Other soul energies have already been through many varied complex experiences and require a very advanced set of experiences in order to gain new growth.

What makes one human life more challenging or advanced for a soul than another human life? Simple. Problems. Give me a human life with many difficult endless problems, and "bingo" you have a very advanced life opportunity for an advanced soul to be challenged. The more successive difficult problems a human life has, the more challenging and interesting it is for the soul. That is a key point I just made, in that more problems, and difficulty means a higher level of interest for the soul. A soul wants interesting experiences. Numerous complex and difficult problems offer the soul a large amount of challenge that make the life experience so much more interesting. The more interesting a life experience is for a soul, the more valuable it is to the soul because it means learning, growth, and evolution is happening at a faster rate. So, from a soul's point of view, a difficult life is a good thing. Chew on that for a bit.

But I do not think that is the only factor. Another major factor is, wait for it: The Hunter Equation! Your life equation probably dictates most of your difficulty level. Let us look at that in detail.

If I am a human embarking on a life, I start to fill in my Hunter Equation. I choose my Future Outcome. What I choose will affect the difficulty level of my life. If I choose a Future Outcome that is unrealistic or impossible, I may be in for a very rough life. If I choose a Future Outcome that is possible, but fraught with problems, then I am also in for a rough life. Here is an example. If I choose my Future Outcome as becoming head of a gang, that choice is likely to bring me some pretty horrible problems and bad consequences. So that would be an example of picking a bad Future Outcome goal.

But really, the equation can go wrong at any point. I may choose a Future Outcome but have a very bad Intent for my choice. Perhaps my Intent is full of hate and revenge. That bad Intent is likely to bring me problems.

If I choose Actions which are very bad choices, those Actions can create very severe consequences and problems. Also, keep in mind that there is often a "snowball effect" or "domino effect" in that one bad choice in the beginning, can affect you and your equation for years to come, and maybe your entire life. So, choosing wrong Actions can certainly result in a human having a very rough life full of nothing but problems.

A person can also be the victim of harsh External Forces that can cause endless problems in their life. Perhaps the person is working for a Future Outcome and taking Actions that are in alignment with very difficult and harsh External Forces. For example, if my Future Outcome is to have my own department store next to Walmart, and I buy a building next to Walmart to start my store, I am likely to have very harsh External Forces hit me as Walmart rolls over me like I'm an ant, and I lose everything. That would be an example of me making choices that put me squarely and predictably in alignment for harsh External Forces to hit me. Try to avoid that.

Conversely, some people may live easy blessed lives from their intentional or accidental equation choices. For example, perhaps someone decides to become a computer programmer, and in doing so takes the Action of going to a particular University. At that University, they meet and fall in love with someone who turns out to be a very wealthy person. The wannabe computer programmer no longer needs to work for a living and lives out their life in luxury. You can see in this example, the person made some logical good choices in their equation that did not hurt things, but really, they hit the lottery in that the Random Luck factor played in their favor and showered them with nothing but wonderful External Forces, which resulted in an even better Future Outcome than they could have hoped for.

The flip side of course, is that one of the major reasons people face problems is because of bad luck. That pesky Random Luck element is in everyone's equation and does not always smile upon us. Some people just experience bad luck and there is not much that can be done to avoid it. That is why those other motivational spiritual concepts such as Law of Attraction, do not have the Random Luck factor within them, because it's too depressing. However, this book is about practical reality and how things really work, so we must be brave and face reality together, okay?

So, if you are a person who has constant problems in their life, consider what I have said above. First, look carefully at your equation to see if you have chosen difficult roads through your own choices. Check to see if you have made bad choices that you can change. Realize that luck plays a part. But if you see nothing wrong with your equation, then it could be that you have a very advanced experienced soul that requires a very advanced human life in order to evolve.

If you determine your soul may be exactly this type, then your only choice is to embrace it and own it. Realize that you are being challenged because it is the only way for you to learn, grow, and evolve quickly. Appreciate the fact that although your life is not easy, your life is full of depth and growth. You can feel it. All of us who have had difficult lives know the secret deep inside, that we have more depth. It is a badge of honor. It is also proof that everything I have said above is true. It is proof that difficult experiences do indeed result in a deeper learning experience that results in a deeper more complex understanding of life. Your soul thanks you.

CHAPTER 24

Ascension

What is Ascension? Wikipedia defines Ascension as: The belief in some religions that there are certain rare individuals that have ascended into Heaven directly without dying first.

In a purely religious sense, Ascension refers to someone who is so pure and worthy, that they gain entry into Heaven without having to die. Obviously, an honor which no human is worthy of, since all humans are sinners according to Christian beliefs. Other religions may look upon the subject differently and have their own specific view as well.

I want to discuss Ascension from a spiritual viewpoint. However, we will still use the official definition, and even the religious views, in our discussions.

So, let's look at this again. Ascension allows you access to Heaven without dying. What does that mean? Well, "Heaven" is the Universe Energy Collective, right? Heaven is where all the Soul Energy goes after it leaves a body. So that is back up into the Universe Energy Collective. That is back home to God, to be with all the other Soul Energy. To be surrounded by love.

So how can a person gain access to the Universe Energy Collective without being dead? I personally do it all the time. But then again, I'm psychic. As a supposedly living person, I "Ascend my mind" into the Universe Energy. I tune into that energy. I can sense, feel, and communicate with Souls that have left bodies after death, and returned to the Universe Energy. In that way, I am visiting Heaven. But I am visiting as only a temporary guest with limited access.

That is more of a spiritual spin on religious ascension. Now let us talk about spiritual ascension. Spiritual ascension is actually quite different. Confused yet? Basically, I am giving you two very different definitions of ascension in the same chapter so that you can understand what ascension means when someone says it, but also recognize you need to know who is saying it in order to know which meaning to apply. Still confused? That is okay.

Let's try to clear up some of the confusion by talking about Spiritual Ascension. Spiritual Ascension is the process of shedding your "old self" and ascending to a higher vibration of existence. So, with spiritual ascension, we are not talking about going to heaven without dying. We are talking about the spiritual process of working on one's "self" so that our thinking is on a higher vibrational level than what it was previously. Some spiritual people refer to it as "awakening."

But what does vibrational level, or a higher vibration mean? Your vibration refers to your level of living and thinking, based upon how much you apply love to your equation. I say this because love is the ultimate ingredient. So, the higher amount of love you incorporate in all your thinking, the higher your vibration frequency will be.

So those people who shed their psyche of anger, resentment, and fear, and replace their thinking with love, are engaging in spiritual ascension.

Thus, a spiritual awakening, or spiritual ascension, is shedding your psyche of those old human vulnerabilities, and replacing them with an evolved view that is based more on love. Doing this raises your vibration, or vibration frequency. Raising your vibration results in a more peaceful, happier, spiritual existence, and promotes the overall evolution of humanity.

As you can see, I have found a way to make both definitions of ascension work. The religious definition of ascension still applies because psychics are able to visit the ascended world in a virtual way even though they are alive. But the definition of ascension you should be concerned about going forward is the spiritual ascension definition.

If you want to evolve, you can engage in ascension to shift your thinking more into patterns of love. What I mean by this is approaching your conflicts with people, your decisions, and your actions, more out of a place of love.

If you disagree with someone, instead of becoming angry and resentful about it, step back and accept the person is in a certain place spiritually and physically, where they feel a certain way about something. Love that person enough to accept their point of view, and then step back from them if you wish.

Approaching conflicts from love does not mean agreeing with someone. It only means accepting that is how they feel, and respecting and loving them enough to allow for that acceptance. Agree to disagree, while wishing them well and hoping they eventually experience growth, education, and evolve from their current position.

Making this shift into approaching everything from love is very difficult, takes lots of self-work, and practice. But a person who has ascended has truly evolved.

CHAPTER 25

Evolution

When most people think of Evolution, they think of the gradual process of human development. For example, they think of Apes becoming Humans, as we know them today. This is not a scientific book on human biology or development. Instead, we are going to discuss Evolution from a psychological and spiritual point of view.

With that said, the human species is about 200,000 years old. However, humankind is thought to have reached its "maturity" 50,000 years ago. So, humanity as we know it is about 50,000 years old. But not really. We can all see that humanity has changed noticeably even in the last 200 years.

My belief is that humanity is evolving on an exponential scale. Perhaps not much evolution occurred thousands of years ago. But as time has gone on, evolution has gradually increased in speed and development.

I believe a primary reason for this, is out of necessity. The Universe and Mother Nature tends to put things in motion when they are necessary, as if it knows when something is needed. This is not surprising, since the Universe is actually intelligent with all that Universal Energy within it.

Perhaps the Universe and the Earth are conspiring to increase the speed of human evolution in an effort to save humanity and the Earth. I think it is safe to say that the answer to human survival is evolution. Humans either evolve out of their self-destructive ways, or they will become extinct.

A humanity with a "Lord Of The Flies" mentality, mixed with powerful destructive technology, is pretty much a recipe for extinction. So, the only answer is for humanity to evolve out of the 'Lord Of The Flies' tribalism mentality.

I judge human evolution by how people treat each other, such as people's level of empathy for each other. Are humans ready to stick a knife in each other's back for the smallest profit, or are people willing to cooperate with each other for the good of the whole?

However, if you did not catch it, what I said in all the paragraphs above is a bit of a paradox, or conflicting. Why would humans evolve out of their current self-destructive behavior, when humans actually evolved INTO their current self-destructive behavior? In other words, humans were creatures living amongst the flora and fauna, and then evolved into very technologically advanced beings that then began exhibiting very destructive psychological behavior. The destructive psychological behavior would be humans destroying the Earth (that sustains them) and destroying each other out of cruelty and tribalism.

So, has evolution been kind to humans? I would say not. It seems to me an existence of living with the Earth, and then transitioning to an existence of killing the Earth, is not a positive evolutionary direction. Furthermore, we have only seen an increase in violent tribalism between different human groups. Humans seem to hate each other more now than 5,000 years ago I would hypothesize. The reason for this is likely competition for declining resources, within an increasing over-population.

Humans have done the worst possible job managing their species and environment. Logic would say you need to increase the output of your resources, while decreasing your population. Humans have done the exact opposite. Humans are on a death march to see how quickly they can over-populate, while destroying the Earth and its resources at the same time.

I would say the evolution of humans over time has been a failure. Yes, we walk upright, communicate with sophisticated languages, and have I-Phones, but we have not evolved at all when it comes to human empathy, compassion, and cooperation. In fact, there would be some people reading this, and laughing at me, as if these traits I just mentioned above are stupid bleeding heart BS. Thus, the positive psychological and behavioral traits humans need for peace, prosperity, and survival, are not valued as much as they should be.

Humans have done a fair job at evolving technologically (for human standards maybe) but have ceased to evolve psychologically. This has resulted in a catastrophic apocalyptic situation that is playing out in super slow motion before our eyes, as we purposely destroy ourselves.

So, my focus is not on how far humans have evolved physically or technologically, but rather how humans are evolving psychologically and intellectually. This evolution, however slow, is critical for human survival long term.

I personally have seen what I feel could be some recent evolution in this area. While I have seen older generations act with complete lack of empathy and with a multitude of greed, I have seen evidence of children and young people seeming less interested in the game of greed. I think somehow in our psyches and DNA there is a shift to a kinder lighter existence. Only time will tell as Millennials become older.

Many people criticize that Millennials are more dependent on outside help and feel a sense of entitlement to receive such help. I would agree. But this thinking also supports the idea that Millennials lean more toward people supporting each other, than it leads to a greedy "winner take all" attitude of older generations. Millennials are also accused of not working as hard as older generations. However, Millennials tend to be more creative, and kind, in place of that. Some would say this is an indication of evolution.

Humanity could be evolving away from an individuality "take what you can for yourself" mindset, and more into a "what works for everyone" mindset. Most Millennials would not think of hoarding food and letting everyone else starve. Yet, some of our older generations were guilty of doing just that not so long ago. I think we have moved beyond that by a slight degree, just in my lifetime. I call that evolution.

In the spirit of adding variety to the conversation, I would also suggest a possible sign of evolution is the seeming increase of psychic and empathic humans. Although hard to prove scientifically, most would agree there seems to be an increase of children who exhibit psychic and empathic abilities. Is this because there is some alien DNA influence? Of is this because there is some influential evolutionary push? Or is it simply because we never noticed psychic children before? I prefer to believe that the Universe is finally encouraging evolution by introducing this sizeable increase in sensitive, empathic, psychic children, many of which are young people and adults now. This sign of evolution is especially important and notable because it is boosting a human's capacity for empathy, which has been sorely lacking.

Conversely, I would introduce a cynical viewpoint for discussion. As I have put forth in the beginning of the book, I believe everything is a sphere, round, and goes in circles and cycles. I would suggest the possibility that Evolution itself does the same thing.

Perhaps evolution really does go in circles. For example, we start as a very primitive species living in caves and playing with rocks. We evolve into a technologically advanced society. But then, due to our immature psychological development, we essentially destroy ourselves. At this point, perhaps if any of our species survives, we are then brought back to living in caves and playing with rocks again. I certainly hope evolution is not a circle, but I feel we should consider that possibility.

But for now, let us go with the assumption that evolution does seem to be proceeding forward in some way. Evolution has been slow, yet I think it has dramatically picked up speed. Now the question to be asked is, how should humans evolve? In what direction? And what is the most efficient way of evolving at the quickest rate?

I think the simple answer is that humans should evolve in order to survive. I do not see humanity surviving without humanity evolving, as I said earlier. So, survival should be the primary reason we can all agree on for evolving.

In which direction we evolve, is up for debate. Some would say stronger and more powerful, while others would say kinder and more intelligent. Humans will argue about this over the foreseeable future. But it seems to me the most logical direction to evolve in would be the direction that secures the longest most solid future for humanity. The second factor might be the direction that gives humans the highest quality of life. But again, humans will argue over that.

One thing we know is that the quickest way to evolve is through education, experience, and thought. Humanity must value education above everything else, engage in as many experiences as possible, and give individual thought and contemplation to all of life's questions.

If humanity violates any part of that equation above or is lacking or slow with any parts of that, then evolution will be slowed. Making education a lower priority will surely slow down evolution. Keeping humans in tribes, rather than providing cultural experiences, will surely slow evolution. Not teaching humans how to think individually will surely slow evolution.

Humanity itself has control over how fast evolution occurs. Everyone reading this can make their own judgments on how we are doing with all that.

One question I would leave you with is, how will you choose to evolve? As an individual, you can choose if you evolve, in what

166

direction, and how you will achieve it. Are you happy with how you are now? Or would you prefer to evolve further? In what direction shall you evolve? Are you willing to take the actions, and put the work into evolving? All questions for contemplation.

One thing for certain, is that evolution is a key factor in human development and survival.

CHAPTER 26

The Ideal Human

There is no ideal human. Meaning, there is no one exact human that is ideal. The reason is that what is ideal would be in the eye of the beholder. We all have our opinions and preferences of what would be ideal. Certainly, this is true in dating, and it is just as true in looking at ideal human creatures.

In addition to the above, we do not want one exact type of ideal human. If we had that, then there would be no variety. Humans love variety (or should). We want different kinds of people. We need variety for a healthy interesting society.

So why am I even writing a chapter titled this way? Because despite what I just said above, there are some basic traits that the ideal human would have. Therefore, I am going to talk about some of those ideal traits that an ideal human would have. I just wanted to make it clear that I am not saying there is only one particular "ideal human race" or such. I am not going there, and neither should you. This chapter is about taking an evolutionary direction toward human traits that maximize success and happiness of humanity. All of these traits can come in all colors, sizes, shapes, national origins, religions, genders, sexualities, and the like. I am suggesting positive evolution to develop ideal traits within everyone, while keeping everyone in all their multiple different styles, personalities, and everything I mentioned above.

The ideal human would have a lot of empathy. High on the empathy scale. If 1 is no empathy and 10 is crying for every squirrel who loses a nut, let us say a 7 on the empathy scale might be nice. Empathy will be the key to human survival. Without all humans having an adequate amount of empathy, we will hate each other, fight, make each other suffer, and eventually snuff each other and ourselves out.

The ideal human would have no need or desire for tribalism. An ideal human would have strong independent values, opinions, thoughts, and positions. They would not need to be led by a group or told who to like and who to hate. Tribalism would be seen as "3rd grade" to an ideal human.

Along the same lines, an ideal human would have high levels of compassion. When someone needs uplifting, the ideal human would be willing to assist and uplift the person in need. Respecting and caring for those less fortunate would be an important and respected part of our society. It creates a sense of security, respect, and caring within a society.

An ideal human is educated and capable of clear reasoning without the interference or help of others. By educated I mean the ideal human understands facts based on reality and science. They understand factual events in reality, not those told to them in fantasy, or with some political or religious agenda. An educated person sees things through clear glasses without filters. An ideal human is capable of learning and using reason to find answers to questions.

An ideal human is capable of thinking in a clear logical way, free from red herrings, subjective opinions, and biased news. An ideal human understands the process of gathering facts, sorting them, determining a correct answer, and then presenting the correct answer.

Additionally, the ideal human is also capable of creativity. Thinking outside the box. Being innovative. The ideal human can use an existing base of knowledge to then come up with a new way of solving a problem or handling a situation. Creativity also in the form of arts for variety and interest would also be valued.

This leads us to the obvious skill of being able to solve problems. The ideal human can be given a problem or obstacle and is able to calmly and efficiently produce a workable solution. This requires education, logic, reasoning, creativity, and a good temperament. Problem solving is critical for human survival.

The ideal human is very proficient at effective communication. The ideal human can fully express their feelings, opinions, ideas, and detailed procedures. It is surprising how many humans today cannot do this well.

The ideal human would have their full range of human emotions, even intense human emotions, but still have them under adequate control. Having emotions under adequate control is necessary for good social interactions, communication, and good decision-making skills. We all know that when our emotions run out of control, we do stupid things we regret, and say stupid hurtful things we regret.

I referenced this earlier, but it bears repeating, the ideal human is able to think independently. The ideal human is able to maintain their own value system and opinions without being told how to think or what to think. This prevents brainwashing and manipulation. If every human were able to think independently, many of our world problems would be solved. This is a critical future skill but requires a good education so that a person knows how to think and reason on their own.

I could probably continue on, but those are a lot of traits I have mentioned above. What do you think? It seems to be regardless of a person's political or religious affiliation, most would agree all of the above traits would be beneficial for humans to have.

So now the fun question. How do you personally measure up to all of the traits mentioned above? Are you strong in many of those traits? Are there some that could use more attention and improvement?

This chapter is not meant to suggest every human be identical and perfect. It is meant to provide a rough template for an evolutionary direction. Are you evolving in the correct direction? Are there things you can work on to evolve more effectively and faster? We could all use this template as a guide to check ourselves.

But while we are working on being the ideal human, do not forget to love and appreciate the unique individuality of who you are now.

CHAPTER 27

The Future Of Humans

The fate of humanity relies on three major factors in my opinion. The first is how well humans evolve in the diminishment of their vulnerabilities. The second is how well humans are able to live in harmony with Earth, rather than destroying it. The third is how well humanity is able to establish adequate levels of empathy within all humans.

Let's start by reminding ourselves of the human vulnerabilities mentioned earlier in the book. They include disease, mental illness, vices, lack of emotional control, need for an Idol, groupthink, greed, and tribalism. Disease and mental illness are somewhat a factor of technological medical advancement. When I say that, I mean both ways, because medical advancements can extend our life, but technological advancements are also contributing to our "self-poisoning" when it comes to our food and over prescribing of medications. In my opinion, medical and technological advancements are not that much of a factor in the survival of humanity. They may be a factor in the life span of each human, but not in the existence of humanity as a whole. Regardless of how and when people die, there are always more humans being born to replace them. The caveat to this is if there is ever a human wide dysfunction in reproduction or DNA. If there is an interruption in human reproduction, it will likely be caused by humans themselves, somehow poisoning themselves to the point of destroying their ability to reproduce with healthy DNA. Vices such as smoking, drinking alcohol, illicit drugs, addictive use of prescription drugs, and such, are all factors in limiting individual life spans. The risk to humanity as a whole would be if there is some substance that comes into being, resulting in a pandemic of addiction that wipes out humans on a large scale.

Lack of emotional control is a tricky one because having many varied emotions is part of the human experience. Yet, not being able to control those emotions can result in very bad decisions, actions, and outcomes. I truly believe that humans will have to strike a better balance between having human emotions to enjoy life as a human vs. controlling those emotions better as to not lead humanity down dangerous paths. Emotions of Love rarely go wrong unless combined with insanity, but emotions of anger, hate, and jealousy, can lead humans to do horrible things. All it will take is one angry hate filled human to develop a new super weapon in his garage, and they could possibly be a real threat to humanity. Controlling one's extreme emotions is critical.

A human's need for an idol is a double-edged sword. On one hand, an idol can be very inspirational to a human and provide direction in life. On the other hand, an idol diminishes a human's individuality and ability for independent thought and contemplation. A human tends to rely completely on their idol for all moral leadership. This can be dangerous if for some reason the idol goes rogue in a destructive direction. It will become critical for humans to begin weaning themselves off depending on idols, and more reliant on critical inward moral analysis and thinking. A group of humans all being led to the same ill-advised direction can be catastrophic, whereas all humans having individual thoughts, creates a check and balance so that if one human goes rogue, the rest are there to stop him.

This leads to the whole issue of groupthink. As stated above, groupthink is very dangerous because it eliminates all checks and balances. It creates a circumstance where one person, or idol, is able to control the thoughts and actions of the masses. The best example of this would be Hitler and the Nazi movement. Germans became so fixated on their leader that they were literally blind to the human atrocities being committed. It is absolutely necessary that humans eliminate groupthink in order to avoid such mass hysteria and catastrophe in the future.

I would say one of the most devastating vulnerabilities in existence is greed. Greed is a vulnerability that all humans possess to some degree. Yet greed is a quality that is never good. Greed, by its nature and by default results in inequality and unfairness. The concept of balance is important in all parts of the Universe, especially in the human psyche and in Mother Nature. Greed specifically seeks out to destroy any sense of balance by causing humans to artificially attain more for themselves than is needed. Greed at its core causes humans to hoard resources, even if other humans die without those resources. Greed justifies injustice, suffering, and death inside a human's mind by making them think it is good to "have more." Greed is so ingrained into the human psyche that it seems almost impossible to think it will ever be eliminated. Yet greed is among the most dangerous of all human vulnerabilities and its elimination or control is critical to the long-term survival of humanity.

Along with greed, tribalism is among the most dangerous of all human vulnerabilities. Tribalism is this mode of thinking where humans must band together into groups, so they can oppose other groups. A human's urge to do this supersedes all logic and common sense. Tribalism is what creates wars. Humans end up no longer thinking with reason or logic. Humans only think in terms of what their tribe needs or thinks. With tribalism, humans often do not even know why they are fighting, or what they are fighting for. That in itself is somewhat a definition of insanity. The insanity of taking positions and actions without even knowing why. Tribalism can literally make people seem insane and act in insane ways. That makes tribalism likely the most dangerous of all human vulnerabilities, and the most likely vulnerability to destroy humanity. Evolving beyond tribalism will be necessary or humanity will not survive. This is especially true with the technological existence of super weapons.

As you can see, human vulnerabilities are a factor for the future of humanity on a sliding scale, with some not as much a critical factor, while others absolutely critical to the eventual survival of humanity. It is up to humanity to either evolve and curb the most critical vulnerabilities or face the consequences.

Logically, some of these human vulnerabilities, such as greed, are causing our second major factor in the survival of humanity, which is our relationship with Earth. Humans are destroying the Earth. Humans are using Earth's resources faster than they can be replaced and polluting the air and water to the point of actually changing the climate. Greed is so strong with humans, there are people who are literally blind to science and facts, just so they can continue polluting the Earth for monetary gain. I am not making any political statement here. I am just stating an objective fact.

What makes our relationship with Earth so interesting is that not very long ago, humans were living in harmony with the Earth. Humans lived close to the Earth and appreciated the cycle and balance between plants, animals, environment, weather, and humans, all living together to provide life. But once the industrial age hit, and humans could exploit the Earth's resources for monetary profit, the balance was destroyed. Profit is much more important to humans than most anything else.

Now we live in a wasteland. Many animals are extinct or scarce. Some fish are too poisonous with mercury and radioactivity to eat, and there is literally garbage floating in the ocean on a grand scale. Then of course, there is the fact that we are cutting trees down and clearing land on a grand scale. Add to that the fact we are dumping poisonous chemicals into our streams and rivers. Water in some communities is now literally poison. Due to all the air pollution, temperatures are rising, ice caps are melting, and the weather is changing in a violent destructive direction. We are literally killing the Earth, and the consequences are biting back. It will only get worse.

Thus, if humans do not kill themselves first, they could become extinct once the Earth is no longer able to support the population. Once our resources are gone, all food sources poisoned, water poisoned, and the environment no longer suitable for human life, the game is over.

It will be critical for humans to reel in their behavior of destroying the Earth. It's really that simple. I am not saying that everyone needs to plant a tree today. I am just saying humans need to *stop* further polluting and destruction. If we simply *stop* the current damage, the Earth will likely regenerate, and all will be fine. Humans absolutely must live in harmony with Earth. There is no negotiation on this one.

But human vulnerabilities and living in harmony with the Earth are not the only factors in the future of humanity. Equally important to our immediate safety, survival, and harmony, is the factor of Empathy within humans. Empathy is a human's ability to understand another human on the deepest level, such that a person can step into that person's shoes and truly feel what they are feeling. Empathy is true understanding.

Humans possess empathy on a sliding scale. Some humans have almost no empathy. These people are sociopathic and think nothing of doing horrible cruel things to other people. They do not think of other humans as people, but rather think of others as objects. They would think of a homeless person as a dirty piece of garbage, or think nothing about torturing animals, or torturing other people for that matter. Those with no empathy have no ability to understand other humans. For this reason, they are capable of the most horrific acts. Hopefully you are getting the picture of how terrifying this is. There truly is nothing more frightening than a person with no empathy, as they will kill and destroy without hesitation, thought, or regret. They have no regret or feelings because they have no empathy.

Contrasting that, are those with an over excessive amount of empathy. Those with an excess of empathy tend to be overly sensitive toward everything. They feel sorry for a tree being cut down. They might have a meltdown if they accidentally run over a squirrel. These people have an overwhelming desire to help any person in need, even at their own expense. They would give the shirt off their back or their last dollar to someone who needed it more than them. People with an excessive amount of empathy forsake themselves and put themselves at risk to help others.

Those with an excessive amount of empathy make horrible landlords because they would let everyone stay for free. They also would make horrible bosses because they would never terminate or discipline anyone that needed it for the sake of the business. I believe the term "bleeding heart liberal" would have come from the existence of such a person with an over-abundance of empathy.

Obviously and hopefully, most people are somewhere in the middle. A balance of empathy is required for a healthy prosperous life. It is not good to be a monster with no empathy, but it is also not good to cry every time a blade of grass is cut, and to forsake all your own necessary needs for the benefit of a random stranger.

The true danger in humanity is the existence of those with no empathy. They are the true destroyers of the world. However, just as important to point out is the existence of those with a tiny bit of empathy, who tend to be the enablers of those with no empathy.

A monster with no empathy will appear strong as steal to his followers. His followers respect this strength. The monster will ruthlessly show his strength by executing, terminating, or punishing people for reason or no reason. The followers will deep down inside be terrified of this and might even know it is wrong. But they will allow the monster to do it because the monster may have convinced them it's for the greater good. Or, the followers might be too scared of the monster, or the followers respect the monster for being so strong and wish they were equally as strong.

People with very little empathy can easily brush aside any empathy they may have had. For example, only a monster with no empathy would send innocent humans to the gas chamber for no reason. But a person with little empathy would follow the orders they are given by simply not thinking about what they are doing. They might have a small amount of empathy, but it is small enough where they can set it aside and not think about it.

A person with adequate amounts of empathy is unable to set their empathy aside. They would be unable to carry out the orders against the innocent people because they would identify with those persecuted personally. A person with adequate amounts of empathy thinks of themselves as being in the other person's shoes. A person with empathy treats others the way they would like to be treated. A person with adequate empathy rescues others if they themselves would want to be rescued under the same circumstances.

A person very high on the empathy scale will risk their own life to save a stranger. They would go out of their way to give blood or donate organs. People high on the empathy scale find it necessary to go above and beyond the call of duty for others because they truly feel the pain of other people. People with high empathy can easily spot someone in pain having a bad day, while those lower on the empathy scale walk right by the person in pain without even noticing.

So how is humanity as a whole balancing empathy at the moment? We see lots of monsters out there with no empathy. We see lots of apathetic people out there with very little empathy, enabling the monsters. We also see people with healthy amounts of empathy, and some light workers with excessive amounts of empathy. Right now, humanity has a very extreme diverse mix. However, humanity also seems to have more people in positions of power who have no or little empathy. This means there might be too many apathetic people with small amounts of empathy who are letting the "monsters" rule.

To me, the future of humanity will depend on how the balance of empathy in our societies shifts over time. If more humans lose their empathy, I believe humanity is certainly doomed. If more humans shift into higher levels of empathy, I believe humanity can survive.

A humanity that loses empathy will see an increase in cruelty. It will see leaders who make choices based on the benefit of a few instead of the majority. Without empathy, all decisions will be based on greed for the few and themselves. Destruction of millions for the benefit of the few will be the mode of thinking without hesitation. This type of mentality will most certainly result in the eventual destruction of humanity, as the most powerful monsters fight each other to the death, while all the innocents are killed as collateral damage. The remaining monster, as victor, will actually self-destruct as his thirst for conquering can no longer continue, and his emptiness inside consumes him until he wilts away and dies without the support of the masses.

Humanity with adequate amounts of empathy will consider the needs of the majority to be the rule, while also leaving nobody behind. An empathic society would not be able to leave the weakest behind, since they would want to be helped if they were in the position of being the weakest. Greed will not be the order of the day because too many people will be thinking of the needs of other people. An empathic society will value peace and prosperity for as many members of their society as possible. Humanity with empathy does a much better job of resolving conflict with others because they are able to put themselves in the shoes of the opposing person. By doing this, communication is enhanced, and both sides are able to work out a peaceful resolution that benefits the most people.

Humanity with empathy is a humanity that operates with love. Anyone who operates with love, is operating under the Universal language of God and the Universe, and thus is in alignment with the Universe as a whole. Anyone who is in proper alignment with themselves, each other, the Earth, the Universe, and God, is likely to live long and prosper.

CHAPTER 28

Your Life, Your Future

When you picked up this book, you may have thought it was going to be just about the Universe, or some equation I made up. But this book is really about you. This book is meant to give you a basic tour around the Universe, life, death, the paranormal, and some new life skills. This book is meant to make your life better.

Hopefully you have a better understanding of how the Universe might work and how we are all connected. But mostly, I hope you take the Hunter Equation and apply it to your life. Apply it to the good, the bad, and the ugly. Life is not easy. Sometimes life is downright scary and unbearable. If you apply your best life skills, along with lots of faith, persistence, and time, you can prevail.

I also talked a lot about evolving, ascending, and great positive traits to have as a person. Perhaps you can be inspired to invest more in yourself, learn, grow, improve, and evolve yourself as you see fit.

Here is my final suggestion to you. First thing to do is take inventory of yourself. What I mean by this is write down all your human vulnerabilities that you feel are a detriment to you now. Then write down where you feel you sit on the empathy scale, from 1 to 10. That gives you a pretty good picture of who you are today.

Then write down who you wish to be. Write down where you think you should be or want to be on the empathy scale from 1 to 10. Then write down which human vulnerabilities you want to get under control, so they are no longer a negative factor in your life. Write down any major life goals you want to accomplish. This gives you a pretty good picture of who you want to be in the future.

So now you have point A and point B. How do you get from point A to point B? Three methods. Through Ascension, Self-Evolution, and by applying The Hunter Equation.

Take the life goals you wrote down and start applying the Hunter Equation to manifest those goals. Each goal would be the Future Outcome, and you know the rest of the process to go through.

Then consider any change you want to make to your level of empathy. Consider any other spiritual or vibrational changes you want to make in your life. Then start to go through Ascension to achieve that new state of mind. Shed the old you and come into the new you. You must admit to who you are, see who you want to be, face your fears, and learn and grow into the new you. Use meditation, reading, exercise, thinking, or any process that works for you.

Then examine all the human vulnerabilities you feel are a problem for you. Decide to evolve out of those. You can even apply the Hunter Equation to change and evolve out of those. But you must do the self-work necessary. It takes time, work, and practice. Each day you can make progress and become a better person. To a large degree, you control your own evolution. So, take control of it. Be the master of your destiny.

If you go through this process I have outlined, you can change yourself, and change your life. You can be whoever you want to be.

You can be a better person. You can be a happier person. You are a critical part of the Universe, and thus you deserve the best the Universe has to offer. You just have to choose to walk toward it and claim it. Much love to you on your journey.

ACKNOWLEDGEMENTS

Thank you Sarah Delamere Hurding
for your editorial assistance,
and your endless support.